TeaTime

TeaTime

A Taste of London's Best Afternoon Teas

Jean Cazals

Foreword by Claire Clark

PAPADAKIS

I would like to dedicate this book to Marie-Ange and Clara whom I love dearly and who are my two life boosters.

I would like to thank Claire Clark and all the people who helped me to make this book successful, especially my publisher Alexandra Papadakis.

I hope this book will encourage even more people to get out and enjoy the wonderful British indulgence of afternoon tea in London whether they live in that city, Paris, New York or Beijing. As you read this book not only will you be able to absorb the atmosphere and consume the cakes, you will also find recipes to make at home.

Long live TeaTime! Long live the spirit of knowing when to stop and reflect on life at TeaTime!

— Jean Cazals

First published in Great Britain in 2012 by Papadakis Publisher

An imprint of New Architecture Group Limited
Kimber Studio, Winterbourne, Berkshire, RG20 8AN, UK

Tel. +44 (0) 1635 248833
info@papadakis.net
www.papadakis.net

Publishing Director: Alexandra Papadakis
Design Director: Aldo Sampieri
Editor: Sheila de Vallée
Editorial Assistant: Juliana Kassianos
Researchers: Juliana Kassianos, Caroline Kuhtz

ISBN 978 1 906506 22 3

All photographs taken in the book were shot using a Panasonic Lumix G3 camera.

A CIP catalogue of this book is available from the British Library.

Printed and bound in China

Contents

FOREWORD

When Jean told me he was doing a book showcasing TeaTime in some of London's wonderful hotels and bijou cafés, I confess I was excited. I'm British, addicted to Early Grey tea and I'm a pastry chef – naturally it's my favourite meal of the day!

More than that, I couldn't wait to see Jean's stunning photography. He's a fantastic food photographer and no stranger to the world of chocolate and cakes, having worked with many great chefs, including the French chocolatier Jean-Paul Hévin. I was lucky enough to work with Jean, too, on my own book *Indulge*, and I'm still in awe of how his artistry provided the visual touchstone for my recipes.

And it's good to have converted a French colleague to a very intrinsic British pleasure. Having a cup of tea with a cake or two around 4pm is such a tradition in our isles. It's part of our cultural DNA and a habit we've exported around the world, yet we only invented the custom about 160 years ago. Actually, Anna Duchess of Bedford (one of Queen Victoria's ladies-in-waiting) is said to have created afternoon tea in the mid-1800s, to stave off that "sinking feeling" between lunch and dinner. What a clever woman. Where she led, royalty and the rest of us followed.

We're still following her example, no more so than in London. You don't have to look far before you find amazing places where you can sip tea and feast on perfect pâtisserie and mouth-watering little sandwiches: from grand or boutique hotels, to chic bars or cafés. They're all in here, in this delicious book. Take my advice and sit back and let Jean lead you on a sumptuous journey round fifty of London's unique and brilliant tea-hotspots.

Better still, give yourself a treat and visit them – all fifty and more, even if it takes a whole year of indulging in a delicious slice of British culinary and cultural heritage.

Claire Clark, chef-pâtissier, London

L'ATELIER DE JOËL ROBUCHON

A great advantage of the intense reds and blacks of Covent Garden's L'Atelier de Joël Robuchon is that once inside you feel completely insulated from the outside world. It is hard to imagine that you are only metres from the theatres and bars of Cambridge Circus.

From the ground floor counter tables, you can watch the highly efficient choreography of the kitchen assembling the meals. The Salon Bar, where you can expect to take your "afternoon indulgence" may not give you the same insight into the creations that the ground floor counter seat might offer, but its crimson and ebony warmth compensate for this with a sense of art-deco luxury that is reflected in the afternoon fare.

Joël Robuchon is one of the world's leading chefs, and his reputation for delivering intricacy, delicacy and flavour is reflected in the "indulgence", a very French interpretation on the English afternoon tea. Fine tarts and traditional dishes are served with a new twist (accompanied by a choice of teas, infusions or "Le marché sans alcool" juice cocktails). But it's called the Salon Bar after all, so perhaps the sexiness of the crimson surroundings will entice you to stretch your teatime into a cocktail or two.

13-15 West Street, Covent Garden, WC2H 9NE · www.joelrobuchon.co.uk · 020 7010 8600

Panellets* with Pine Nuts & Anise

Serves 15

Marzipan

500g ground almonds
Zest of 1 lemon
250g caster sugar
4 eggs

Pine nuts

Mix the ingredients together to make a homogeneous paste.

Roll the paste into small balls of about 15g each.

Roll the balls in the pine nuts.

Put them in the oven at 190°C until they are golden (about 2 minutes).

To serve

Anise liqueur

Remove from the oven and pour a little anise liqueur over them.

*A traditional Catalan dessert eaten on All Saints' Day.

BAR BOULUD

MANDARIN ORIENTAL

F amous for having the best burger in town, this hugely popular lunch and dinner venue has now added afternoon tea to its repertoire. Located in the den-like, wine-cellar-inspired room under the Mandarin Oriental, and opened in 2010, this is where Knightsbridge ladies come to gossip over copious glasses of Champagne, where big money deals are brokered over plates of charcuterie, and dazed tourists come to escape the mayhem of nearby Harrods and Harvey Nichols. Surrounded by interesting 'wine stain' art – depicting Lyon-born chef Daniel Boulud's favourite wines – and Adam D. Tihany chandeliers, it is not the most obvious place for tea. However the delicious offerings should not be ignored. With a bespoke circular cake stand, the tea kicks off with sandwiches containing the famous Bar Boulud hams, including Jambon de Bayonne and Jamón Ibérico. Less carnivorously inclined patrons can feast on the cucumber and cream cheese instead. Pastries include Earl Grey éclairs and a moist Black Forest gâteau, and there are also feather-light madeleines and scones. Wash it down with a glass of Champagne or one of the many teas on offer, from citrusy leaves of Provence, to floral Formosa Oolong, or a herbal infusion such as fresh ginger or lotus flower. Enough to restore even the most weary of shoppers.

66 Knightsbridge, SW1X 7LA · www.mandarinoriental.com · 020 7201 3899

Apple, Caramel & Almond Cake

Serves 20

Almond sponge

430g almond paste
455g whole egg
60g sugar
150g butter
150g soft flour
6g baking powder

Cream the almond paste and sugar in a mixer.
Slowly incorporate the egg and mix to ribbon stage.
Then incorporate the melted butter followed by the dry ingredients.
Spread out onto baking trays about 6-8 mm thick and cook at
175°C for 7 minutes.

Apple caramel

1kg sugar
300g butter
400g bramley apples,
cored and chopped

Cook the sugar and butter to a golden caramel.
Turn off the heat and incorporate the apple.
Turn the heat back on to dissolve the caramel and cook the apples.
Once the apples are tender cover with cling film and leave to cool and infuse.
After 20 minutes pass through a sieve and set aside.

White chocolate cream

200g milk
10g glucose
340g white chocolate
400g whipping cream

Melt the chocolate over a water bath.
Boil the cream and glucose.
Make an emulsion with the chocolate and cream.
Using a hand blender, blitz in the cold whipping cream and put aside in the
fridge overnight to allow the chocolate to crystallise.

To serve

Cut the almond sponge into 4 rectangles.
Warm the apple caramel to about 40°C (this will allow it to soak into the sponge).
Layer up the pastry starting with a rectangle of sponge, then the caramel, and
repeat. Once 4 layers have been completed, put in the fridge for about 1 hour.
Cut the sponge to the required size. And finish with the white chocolate cream.

BEA'S OF BLOOMSBURY

For a long time, Theobald's Road was a faceless thoroughfare, between the West End and the City. But it was here, beside the barristers of Gray's Inn, that Virginia-born Bea Vo saw an opportunity to convert a former bank into the sort of café she felt was lacking.

The open-plan kitchen entrances visitors, as they watch the seasonal cupcake selections being assembled – the flavours change daily – think double chocolate fudge, blackberry vanilla and sticky toffee pudding for autumn. Her cupcakes use light Italian buttercream icing, and are beautifully displayed. But that's only the start of the menu. As a former pastry chef at Nobu, Bea is familiar with delicate flavours, but here the delight is in American-inspired, artisanal fare, from apple bread to the crumbly scones served as part of afternoon tea.

The atmosphere in the shop is one of unpretentious indulgence (the mismatched crockery should leave you in no doubt), and the addition of a savoury menu has made it even more popular. Bea has expanded beyond Bloomsbury, with branches in the City and Chelsea, but all of the cakes are made in the original Theobald's Road branch – and that's why it's the one to choose. However, full afternoon teas are served only at weekends with an abbreviated Sweet Tea available on weekdays. Full afternoon tea is available seven days a week at St. Paul's in the City.

44 Theohalds Road, Bloomsbury, WC1X 8NW · www.beasofbloomsbury.com · 020 7242 8330

TEA MENU
Assam Breakfast
Earl Grey
Peppermint
Organic Lapsang
Gunpowder Green Tea
Dragonwell Green Tea
Lemon Verbena
Vanilla Black
Rooibos
Jasmine
Darjeeling

THE BERKELEY

If couture is out of your budget range but you are sartorially inclined, the Prêt-à-Portea is a brilliantly fun way to eat fashionably without breaking the budget. Started eight years ago, the hotel's pastry chefs visit London Fashion Week to get inspiration from the catwalks, and after consulting fashion editors of glossy magazines such as *Vogue* and ELLE, pick the season's top looks. These couture creations are then turned into edible delights. For example, Miu Miu fans can feast on a glittery blue shoe, in the shape of the hit stiletto of the season; and Bottega Veneta's colour blocking can be sampled as a pink and orange mousse, topped with a delicate macaroon. A Valentino clutch bag is artfully transformed into an orange and ginger clutch cake with an oversized bow. Savoury offerings come in the form of miniatures, perfect for the waistline-conscious trendsetter – such as coriander and fennel crusted tuna with plum jam or a beef and rocket wrap. The Champagne tea includes a glass of Laurent Perrier, or you can opt for the Couture Champagnes at extra cost including Billecart-Salmon.

Teas include White Peony, the Berkeley blend, African Amber and Pear Caramel.

This is all served on pretty multicoloured striped bespoke porcelain designed by British tailor Paul Smith and made by Thomas Goode. The collections change twice a year.

Wilton Place, Knightsbridge, SW1X 7RL · www.the-berkeley.co.uk · 020 7235 6000

Chocolate Biscuit (Burberry Prorsum)
Purple Shot (Lanvin)

Makes 25-30 biscuits
Makes 30 shots

Chocolate biscuit

180g butter
70g icing sugar
230g flour
20g cocoa powder
20g egg white
20g melted butter

Mix the butter, icing sugar, flour and cocoa powder together to a crumble.
Add the liquid and mix until it is all incorporated. Chill in the fridge.
Roll out the dough to 2mm thick. Cut the biscuit to the desired shape.
Bake in the oven for 8-10 minutes at 180°C. Then let it cool.
Outline the biscuit with plain white icing then flood it with slightly runny icing.
Let it dry over night, then pipe the details on next day.

Cassis Bavarois

200g milk
200g whipping cream
90g egg yolks
42g caster sugar
13g gelatine sheets
430g cassis purée
255g whipping cream

Bring the milk and cream to the boil then add the yolks and sugar and cook to 82°C.
Add the gelatine, then the purée and pass through a sieve.
Cool the mixture to 30°C then fold in the lightly whipped cream and pour into the shots.

French meringue topping

125g egg whites
250g caster sugar

Whip half of the sugar with the egg whites for a few minutes and then slowly add the rest of the sugar and whip to a stiff peak.
Using a star nozzle pipe onto a tray lined with parchment paper.
Set the oven to 80°C and put the meringue in to dry overnight.

Crème de Mûre jelly

140g blackberry purée
30g Crème de Mûre
11g caster sugar
4.5g gelatine sheets

Soak the gelatine in the Crème de Mûre.
Bring the purée and the sugar to the boil and add the gelatine mixture.
Mix thoroughly, then cool.
Pour on top of the shot filled with the set cassis bavarois.

BOND & BROOK

FENWICK

Since its refit in 2010, Fenwick on Bond Street has become less of a fusty institution and is now a destination which can rightly compete with other neighbouring smart department stores such as Liberty's. As part of its facelift, upmarket caterers Rhubarb have devised a menu for Bond & Brook (so called because the department store is on the corner where both streets meet) that spans breakfast, lunch and tea. Not only is it now a lunch spot for people from many of the surrounding offices and galleries, it is where visiting groups of smartly dressed out-of-towners come with one aim in mind – shopping. Located on the second floor next to the well-laid out women's collections, it is a good way to refuel before blowing the next paycheck. This small but well designed corner café has beautiful square marble tables, grey bucket chairs and a huge sweeping chrome bar. Bibliophiles can browse the numerous fashion books on display, which are arranged on white shelves next to giant bottles of Chanel N° 5.

The menu offers small bites, such as Shepherd's Pie, Crab cakes and Caponata. There is also a full afternoon tea or you can choose just tea and scones. Tea is served in elegant silver pots, and includes Imperial Earl Grey, Orange Blossom Oolong or the tasty Bond & Brook Breakfast Blend. It is also a great place – on the evidence of a few visits – where shopping-phobic husbands or wives can hide for a few hours with a good book.

63 New Bond Street, Mayfair, W1A 3BS · www.fenwick.co.uk · 020 7629 9161

White Chocolate Pannacotta

Serves 6

166g white chocolate

50g caster sugar

366ml double cream

50ml milk

1.5 gelatin sheets

Soak the gelatin sheets in cold water until soft and squeeze out any excess water.

Place the milk and the cream in a saucepan and heat through but do not boil.

Put the gelatin into the cream and stir until dissolved.

Put the chocolate and the sugar into a bowl. Pour the cream mix over the chocolate and stir until the chocolate has melted. Pass the mixture through a sieve and pour into moulds.

Place in the fridge and leave to set.

Once set, dip the mould into warm water for a few seconds to loosen the sides before turning out onto the serving plate.

To serve

Home-made shortbread

Plum jam

Serve with home-made shortbread and a dollop of plum jam.

THE ENGLISH TEA ROOM

BROWN'S HOTEL

This elegant building on Albemarle Street – where Rudyard Kipling allegedly penned *The Jungle Book* – opened its doors in 1837. However, designer Olga Polizzi, creative director of her brother Rocco Forte's hotels (he has owned Brown's since 2005) has ensured that it has kept up with the times.

Although the English Tea Room is still all blazing fireplaces, wood-panelled walls and elaborate cornicing, she has added her famously tasteful contemporary flare. Artworks are by Tracey Emin and Sir Peter Blake with lighting by Paul Smith. The large room offers many warm and inviting corners in which to take tea, aided by the jaunty tunes of the pianist, who plays during the tea service. The health conscious can indulge in their Tea-Tox afternoon tea, which includes tasty morsels such as chicory leaf with smoked mackerel and a soft-boiled quail's egg followed by a selection of sweet treats such as sea buckthorn jelly. For a more gluttonous blowout the Champagne Afternoon Tea is a classic way to while away a few hours if you are out and about in Mayfair. There are two tea sommeliers to advise on the seventeen teas on offer. If you wish your experience to extend beyond afternoon tea, you might want to take part in one of the hotel's Tea-Torials, where head pastry chef Theodore Ndeh teaches the art of the perfect scone followed by tea and questions in the tea room.

Albemarle Street, Mayfair, W1S 4BP · www.brownshotel.com · 020 7493 6020

Honey & Camomile Tea Cake

Serves 12

5g camomile tea

250g butter

180g caster sugar

5 whole eggs

250g self-raising flour

50g honey

Pinch of salt

Take the camomile tea, place in a blender and blend until it becomes a fine yellow powder.

Sift through a fine sieve and discard the bigger pieces. Reserve until needed in an airtight container.

Cream the butter, sugar, pinch of salt, and camomile. Then add in the eggs slowly, followed by the honey.

Sift the self-raising flour, then fold in to create a smooth mixture.

Pipe into the rectangular mould and bake at 150°C until golden brown.

Take out of the oven and allow to cool at room temperature. Store in the fridge until needed.

To serve

Golden syrup or apricot jam

Honey pollen drops (optional)

Glaze top with golden syrup or apricot jam and sprinkle a few drops of honey pollen drops onto the top of the cake.

BRUMUS
HAYMARKET HOTEL

L ocated a stone's throw from Trafalgar Square, this is a great pitstop from an afternoon of soaking up some culture in the nearby galleries and theatres. Situated in an elegant Regency townhouse, tea can be taken in the light-filled conservatory, or the Brumus Restaurant which is fun and comforting with its bright magenta and purple colour scheme. With a bar at one end and bold art at the other, it is a fun place to let the afternoon fade away and tea is good value when compared with some of the larger hotels. The tea comes on a tiered stand and highlights include giant macaroons and forest fruit tarts with all items replenished free of charge. There is a choice of speciality teas or teas from the Miller Harris range of delicate loose leaf teas: the Bigarade is a full-bodied second flush Assam infused with Brazilian bigarde oil, while for something calmer try the sweet blackcurrant scented Violette. Walk off the afternoon's excesses in nearby St. James's Park.

1 Suffolk Place, Piccadilly, SW1Y 4HX · www.firmdale.com · 020 7470 4000

CHARLOTTE STREET HOTEL

T his perennially popular hotel, always packed to the rafters with surrounding media people, is decked out in the same faultlessly chic way as the others in Kit and Tim Kemp's stable of Firmdale Hotels. A short walk from Tottenham Court Road, it offers a stylish refuge for a few hours. Tea can be taken in the Drawing Room but a more relaxing option is the Library, located past the Reception at the back of the hotel. With its large open fire, massive sofas and kind lighting, it resembles a huge comfy sitting room in a friend's house. Paintings on the wall are by the Bloomsbury Group including Vanessa Bell. The room has clusters of spaces so you can easily while away a few hours with friends without being disturbed.

The teas are seasonal. If you order a Pommery Winter Tea a glass of Pommery NV champagne is followed by a selection of savouries such as turkey and cranberry and cream cheese and beetroot finger sandwiches and a mini sausage roll with apple sauce. Sweet offerings include scones with cream and jam, a chocolate pot with brandy snap, toasted panettone, chestnut mont blanc, and cherry cupcake with sherbet frosting. In summer there is a Pimms Summer Afternoon Tea. Mini croque-monsieurs, mandarin ice-cream shots and chocolate tiffins can be ordered as additional items.

The afternoon tea menu includes a selection of teas, coffees and infusions including peppermint and lime or jasmine iced tea. Speciality teas such as green jasmine flower blossom and wild rooibos can be ordered for a small supplement. A gluten-free option is also available.

15-17 Charlotte Street, Fitzrovia , W1T 1RJ · www.firmdale.com · 020 7806 2000

Fruit Tartlets

Makes 12

Sablé pastry

50g icing sugar
50g butter
125g flour
1 egg
15ml double cream

Place the icing sugar, butter and flour in an electric mixer and mix together.

Add the eggs and double cream to bind the mixture.

In the bowl roll the mixture into a ball and cover with cling film. Place in the fridge and leave for 20 minutes.

Remove the ball and roll out on a floured surface.

Place the pastry over individual metal tart rings and push into the corners making sure the thickness remains the same. Cut the excess away and repeat with the rest of the cases.

Place the rings in the freezer and leave for 5 minutes. Remove from the freezer and bake in a pre-heated oven at 180°C until golden brown.

Remove from the oven and leave to cool. Turn out onto a wire rack. The tart cases should be firm.

Crème pâtissière

150ml milk
2 egg yolks
30g sugar
20g all-purpose flour
1 vanilla pod

Pour the milk into a saucepan and scrape the vanilla pod into the pan.

In a separate bowl cream the egg yolks, flour and sugar together with a wooden spoon.

Place the saucepan on the hob and heat until just at boiling point, remove from the heat.

Add a little of the milk to the creamed mixture and stir. Then return all of the mixture to the pan of milk and stir continuously until the mixture thickens. Leave to cool.

To serve

Fresh fruit

Take the tart cases, fill with the crème pâtissière and top with fresh fruit.

THE CHURCHILL

HYATT REGENCY

Situated a stone's throw from the hub of Oxford Street and Hyde Park with views over the picturesque gardens of Portman Square, the calm and contemporary colours of The Montagu, where afternoon tea is served, create a welcoming and relaxing atmosphere.

The Montagu Afternoon Tea offers elegant tiered stands bearing a traditionally British afternoon tea. For the traditional British sandwiches, the fresh fillings are created to match the mix of white, brown and flavoured (tomato, carrot or rye) bread and change daily. The warm fruit and plain scones are served with strawberry jam and Cornish clotted cream. The Patissier's selection includes pretty French pastries, fruit tartlets and mini desserts, which also change daily. The Montagu Afternoon Tea is served with a selection of exquisite teas including Sapphire Earl Grey, Darjeeling Second Flush, Organic Bohea Lapsang, Organic Silver Needles and Handrolled Jasmine Pearls. And for that extra special treat, guests can also add a glass of the Sommelier's choice of champagne.

There is also a playful Sex in the City tea which includes pastrami on rye, mini burgers and delightful pastries that have been produced with each of the four girls in mind – the most tempting being Carrie's strawberry-flavoured chocolate pink stiletto.

30 Portman Square, Marylebone, W1H 7BH · www.london.churchill.hyatt.com · 020 7299 2037

CLARIDGE'S

As the 2011 winner of the Tea Guild's award for the Top London Afternoon Tea, Claridge's is already established as a not-to-be-missed destination. You can see why as soon as you enter. On passing through the revolving doors you are thrust into the wonderfully grand entrance hall with its smart white and black flooring in keeping with the hotel's Art Deco style. The Foyer, where afternoon tea is served, has a glamour all its own. It was restored by architect Thierry Despont a decade ago with a magnificent silver light sculpture by Dale Chihuly as its centrepiece. The atmosphere is smart, but not stuffy or formal – and made all the more relaxing by the classical pianist playing in the background.

With over 30 teas on offer chosen by Mariage Frères, this is certainly a place to stretch your tea horizons perhaps by ordering the luxurious Royal White Silver Needles. The afternoon tea itself is a traditional affair, with some interesting twists such as their own Marco Polo jelly infused with tea to accompany the scones. It is all served on the exquisite green and white Bernardaud porcelain made specially for the hotel. For very special occasions, the Ruinart Afternoon Tea is a treat.

Brook Street, Mayfair, W1K 4HR · www.claridges.co.uk · 020 7629 8860

Coconut Dacquoise Sous Vide Pineapple

Makes 47

Coconut dacquoise

(6cm x 47 rings)
150g ground almonds
270g icing sugar
80g desiccated coconut
15g Sevarome coconut paste
300g egg whites
100g caster sugar
2.5g dried egg white powder

Sieve the ground almonds and icing sugar together, then add the coconut.

Whisk the egg whites to a meringue with the sugar.

Add a small amount of the egg whites to the coconut paste and mix until smooth.

Fold in the dry ingredients, then fold in the coconut paste.

Line the 6cm tart rings with silicone paper strips 3cm deep.

With a n° 7 nozzle, pipe the dacquoise in a spiral onto the base and pipe bulbs around the outside edge against the paper – approximately 9-10 bulbs.

Bake at 150°C, ½ fan for 20-25 minutes. Allow to cool, demould and remove paper.

Sous vide pineapple

(approximately 70)
1kg 540g of pineapple batons (4cm x 1cm)
1lt stock syrup
20g chopped coriander leaves
50g ginger juice

Peel and grate the fresh ginger, place in muslin and squeeze out the juice.
Remove the coriander leaves from the stalks and chop finely.
In a bowl combine all the ingredients and stir together.
Divide the above into 2 large vacuum bags and vac pac on n° 9.
All the juice should be bubbling very fast. When this is achieved stop the vacuum process and remove the air. Keep in the bags.
Spread flat on a tray and leave overnight in the fridge to infuse the flavours.

Candied ginger

Take the candied ginger and rinse off the excess syrup. Cut in half if too big and slice the ginger.
Keep in the fridge. (The ginger can be sliced and stored in advance).

Calamansi Lime Crémeux

750g whole eggs
800g caster sugar
27g lime zest
535g Calamansi purée
1kg 165g butter, very soft but not melted
9¾ gelatine leaves, soaked in cold water

Bring to the boil eggs, sugar, lime zest and purée whisking all the time.
Pass through a conical strainer and add the soaked gelatine.
Cool to 60°C, add the soft butter and blitz for 3 minutes until smooth and shiny.
Place in vac bags, 1kg 50g per bag.
Freeze until needed.

Drain the syrup from the pineapple and leave to drain dry for around 1 hour at room temperature.
Dust the Dacquoise with neige decor. Place onto gold board.
Pipe a bulb of Calamansi Lime Crémeux in the centre of the dacquoise, add 2 slices of candied ginger and top off with more crémeux.
Heat the reserved pineapple syrup until very hot.
Divide pineapple into small batches and taking 1 batch at a time add the hot glaze and stir in.
Place the sous vide pineapple batons on top of the crémeux and arrange in haphazard fashion.
Place 3 red currants on top with the hairy part against the pineapple to prevent bleeding.

COCOMAYA

Founded in 2008, Cocomaya is the brainchild of Joel Bernstein, former head of concept at Liberty's and accessories designer Walid al Damirji, two of the world of fashion's movers and shakers.

Cocomaya looks as if it has been casually thrown together. The truth is a very different matter. One enters a world of magic in this chocolatier and artisan bakery on Connaught Street. All mismatched vintage teacups and teapots, communal tables, piles of chocolate skulls and wicked cakes. The pink, pistachio, and rough wood-encased rooms are an overpowering experience with aromas of cocoa and baked goodies. All very sensual and affordable luxury. One is always sure to see fashionista royalty and celebrities passing through for lunch, tea, or take-away.

Using only Fair Trade South American cocoa and no preservatives, their inventive chocolate flavours range from sour cherry to lavender to coffee and cardamom. All handmade on site. Afternoon teas are served on antique cake stands with sweet treats including pistachio and rose shortbread or honey-oozing mini cakes. Group tea parties can be arranged but be aware that these are pre-booked weeks ahead of time. This place is a fairy-tale escape for adults and children alike.

Both the chocolates and cakes are for sale to take home and if your craving is for the savoury there is a range of salads, sandwiches, and canapés.

3 Porchester Place, Paddington, W2 2BS · www.cocomaya.co.uk · 020 7706 2770

Kuglof

Serves 14

350g unsalted butter

450g caster sugar

7 eggs

1 vanilla pod

400g plain flour

1 tsp baking powder

1 tsp baking soda

1 tsp salt

300g sour cream

Cream the butter and sugar together until creamy.

Beat in the eggs, followed by the sour cream.

Then sift in the dry ingredients and combine.

Divide mixture between 14 special kuglof tins.

Bake for 30 minutes at 155°C.

COMPTOIR GASCON

If you're visiting the Comptoir Gascon near Smithfield Market for afternoon tea, you may find it hard to imagine that each morning London's meat supply is traded here in a frenzy of activity. However, the action is largely over by 7am. For a long time, once the market had closed the area was largely deserted, and so hopes were not high when Pascal Aussignac opened his restaurant Club Gascon on West Smithfield. However, the ability to recreate the delights of South-West France soon brought it a strong following (and Michelin star), long before Smithfield had the bars and restaurants that make it a popular evening choice for Londoners today. Not long afterwards, he opened the Comptoir Gascon in nearby Charterhouse Street as a delicatessen with a few seats so that you could take home the foie gras and cheeses you had enjoyed in the restaurant. By 2005, dining in the deli was proving so popular that they reduced the shop and expanded the seating to some fifty covers – the Comptoir became the Gascon bistro of choice in London.

Stepping inside the tall entrance, you feel transported. The place has a warm, rustic feel that makes you relax instantly. You can see its delicatessen origins in the hanging hams and the chutneys, confits, chocolate-covered sauterne-infused raisins, and lentils in goose fat lining the shelves in the far corner. Here, too, is the cake display, beside a selection of rustic breads. There's no formal afternoon tea menu, but more than enough on offer for you to create your own indulgence, which is what many regulars do.

63 Charterhouse Street, Clerkenwell, EC1M 6HJ · www.comptoirgascon.com · 020 7608 0851

Chorizo Canelés*

Makes 18

200ml milk
30g butter
50g flour
40g grated cheese
1 egg
50g chopped chorizo
Salt (optional)

It is very important that you use canelé moulds, which are available from specialist kitchen shops.

The first day

In a small saucepan, combine the milk and butter and bring to a simmer.

In the meantime, in a medium mixing-bowl, gently whisk the flour, cheese and egg.

Add the dry mix and the chorizo to the warm milk (you may want to add some salt).

Stir until well combined.

Allow to cool to room temperature, then cover and refrigerate overnight.

The next day

Prepare the moulds for baking by buttering them (if you are not using silicon moulds).

Preheat the oven to 210°C.

Remove the batter from the fridge: it will have separated a bit, so stir until well blended again.

Pour into the prepared moulds, filling them to 2/3 (they will rise when baking).

Put into the oven for 10 minutes at 210°C (make sure you don't open the oven door).

Then remove the moulds and cover with baking parchment.
Put them back into the oven to cook for another 15 minutes at 205°C.

Take out of the moulds straightaway.

The canelés are ready when the bottoms are a very dark brown, but not burnt.

Unmould onto a tray (wait for about 10 minutes first if you are using silicon moulds or they will collapse a little) and serve when they are still hot.

*Chorizo Canelés are unconventional. These little cakes are famous sweet delicacies from the region of Bordeaux, France. The traditional recipe can be found in *Cuisinier Gascon* by Pascal Aussignac.

THE CONNAUGHT

Jam lovers should make a beeline for the elegant Espelette room at the Connaught, where there is London's only fully dedicated jam trolley. Alsace jam maker Christine Ferber's delectable jams are created for her old friend Hélène Darroze, head chef at the Connaught, made with the best pickings from the local harvest. Out of the 800 she has created in her life so far, offerings for the Connaught include cherry, rhubarb and mint, and milk chocolate and raspberry. Offerings such as quince jelly include rose petals from her own garden. Spread these over warmed plain or ginger scones. The light airy room looks out onto Mount Street and the dramatic Tadao Ando water feature. Inside the cream-coloured room, guests can enjoy their tea to the sounds of the resident harpist.

The Chic and Shock tea kicks off with finger sandwiches including smoked salmon and wasabi, terriyaki chicken, grilled Japanese aubergine, and cucumber and dill. Pastries are sumptuous – with more nods to the Orient by Hélène Darroze. Feast on sesame frangipane tarte with yuzu butter or rhubarb compôte with an infusion of Samba jelly and ginger foam. Chocolate lovers will love the chocolate and caramel mousse with a hazelnut dacquoise.

Teas are broken into sections – green (Sencha and Bangkok), black (Ceylon Orange Pekoe and Royal Connaught Afternoon), white (Espelette blend and Silver Needles) and aromatic (Paris and Pomegranate). A perfect pitstop after splurging in nearby Christian Louboutin and Marc Jacobs.

Carlos Place, Mayfair, W1K 2AL · www.the-connaught.co.uk · 020 7499 7070

CORINTHIA HOTEL

hen you enter the grand lobby of the Corinthia Hotel located among the Government offices at the north end of Whitehall, it is hard to imagine that it was, until 2007, a government building. The emphasis here is on luxury and detail.

Afternoon tea is served in the Lobby Lounge, beneath a Baccarat chandelier. Tea is taken very seriously with a tea sommelier on hand to guide you among the impressive selection of Tea Palace teas including Single Estates, Black, Green and White teas, organic herbal infusions, fruit infusions and seasonal teas.

There is a traditional Afternoon Tea and a more luxurious Laurent Perrier Afternoon Tea but it is chef-pâtissier Claire Clark's wide selection of cakes from the delicate to the traditional that make the Corinthia worth a detour. Several of the cakes, available by the slice, can be seen under the glass cloches on the lobby table, complete with accompanying history (what happened in 1820 to create the first Bakewell Tart?) Also available are chocolates by Damian Allsop, famous for using spring water to create a lighter taste that allows the full taste of the underlying chocolate to come through, without the butter and cream predominating – the perfect indulgence at the end of any afternoon tea.

Whitehall Place, Westminster, SW1A 2BD · www.corinthia.com · 020 7930 8181

Coconut Mousse

Serves 12-15

1 egg white

60g caster sugar

18g water

200g 35% UHT whipping cream

250g coconut purée (cap fruit)

3g gelatine

46ml whipping cream

Heat a third of the purée and the UHT whipping cream.

Soak the gelatine in cold water until it is soft.

Once the gelatine is soft squeeze excess water out and add to the purée and whipping cream. Mix well.

Then add the rest of the purée. Mix well and place in the fridge to set.

Soft whip the cream and reserve in the fridge.

Make an Italian meringue by cooking the sugar and water to 121°C.

As the sugar is cooking start to whisk the egg whites.

Pour the cooked sugar onto the meringue and whisk until cold.

Take the purée mix out of the fridge and break it down with a whisk until it is smooth.

Fold in the Italian meringue.

Then fold in the cream.

Pipe into rubber tube mats.

Put in the fridge to firm (approximately 4 hours).

THE CRITERION

During a weekend house party at Blenheim in the 1930s, Lady Astor, the first woman in parliament, was said to have commented to Winston Churchill, "if I were your wife, I'd put poison in your coffee." "Nancy," Churchill is said to have replied, "if I were married to you, I'd drink it." As Churchill was a regular at the Criterion, it might, therefore, be wiser to stick to the tea.

The neo-byzantine opulence of the Criterion Restaurant makes it one of the most impressive venues in London, which might at first seem slightly misplaced amidst the neon consumerism of Piccadilly Circus. But the Criterion more than holds its own, transporting you even more deeply into another era since its refurbishment in 2009. It now seems incredible that this building was once set for demolition. Look up as you enter, and you'll be reminded that the restaurant was established in 1873. Keep looking up, and you'll be entranced by the gold mosaic ceiling and if you look around you by the marble floors, the mirrored walls and the imposing arches.

While the high ceilings and marble columns might not offer the most intimate of settings, the afternoon tea won't disappoint, especially if you opt for the champagne option at the second sitting from 4pm. From here it's not far to the Long Bar and a Leo Engel classic cocktail (named after the Criterion's first head bartender) – I'd suggest the Criterion Reviver. Just watch out for that coffee!

224 Piccadilly, W1J 9HP · www.criterionrestaurant.com · 020 7930 0488

DAYLESFORD ORGANIC FARMSHOP & CAFÉ

W If you want to live the Cotswolds' dream, Daylesford is the place. With its artfully arranged carts of pumpkins, bowls of water for dogs and overflowing displays of seasonal organic vegetables, this is the place to unwind with fellow yummy mummies. Located in the smart villagey neighbourhoods of Notting Hill and Pimlico, this is where you can happily wear your Hunter wellies and bring along your black labrador and brood of Brora-clad children and fit right in. The brainchild of Lady Bamford, whose husband made his fortune with JCB, the heart warming and impeccably chosen products – mostly made on their estate – are hard to resist. Particularly lovely is their range of rose geranium bathroom products.

In Pimlico, the white marble-clad temple to organic temptations offers a tea-room upstairs where leisurely cups of own-brew black or green teas can be taken on beechwood communal tables. Jostle with the smart local set as you savour the individual cakes on offer from Earl Grey fruitcake to a rich chocolate wheat-free cake, lemon or Manuka honey cakes, or scones with cream and jam. Don't miss the surrounding shelves lined with goodies that offer something for everyone, be it your toddler, gardener or beloved pet. The shop downstairs sells wonderful products to take home from ginger snap biscuits to delicious cheeses and organic pressed apple juice.

44b Pimlico Road, Pimlico, SW1W 8LP · www.daylesfordorganic.com · 020 7881 8060

DAYLESFORD ORGANIC FARMSHOP & CAFÉ
Fruit Cake

Serves 15

115g sultanas
115g raisins
115g currants
115g butter (unsalted, softened)
115g caster sugar
3 eggs, beaten
115g self-raising flour
30g candied mixed peel
1 lemon zest

Soak the dried fruit for 3 hours in black tea, drain and then pat dry on a cloth.

Preheat the oven to 170°C.

Grease and line a 9-inch loaf tin, approximately 4-5 inches deep.

In the mixer, cream the butter and sugar together until pale.

Add the eggs, a little at a time, until fully incorporated.

Fold in half of the flour. Then add the soaked dried fruit, candied peel, lemon zest, and the rest of the flour.

Spoon the mix into the tin and bake for approximately 50 minutes. Test that it is cooked through by piercing the middle of the cake with a skewer. It should come out clean.

Turn out of the tin onto a wire rack and allow to cool.

DAYLESFORD
ICE CREAMS
"
- DARK CHOCOLATE
- VANILLA
- GOOSEBERRY
- BUTTERSCOTCH

£3.99 a POT
_____ "

daylesfordorganic
organic drinking chocolate
250g min wt

daylesford...
jasmine pearl tea
loose leaf 200 g ℮

daylesfordorganic
organic morning tea
black tea blend
loose leaf 125g ℮

daylesford...
organic Earl Grey wit...
black tea blend
20 crystal teabags 40...

DEAN STREET TOWNHOUSE

T his hip hotel and media haunt, which opened in 2009, is one of those places in London where you might still find a cracking good lunch morphing seamlessly into dinner. As part of the Soho House Group, this ensures it is always abuzz, mostly with a louche in-crowd who are invariably mixing business with pleasure over endless bottles of wine. However, for those whose cravings are more restrained, it is certainly one of the most stylish places in which to take afternoon tea. Surrounded by works of art from a pantheon of British greats from Tracey Emin, to Peter Blake and Keith Coventry the traditional with a twist room is designed for lounging – deep armchairs invite you to let the afternoon drift away, and in winter, it is lovely to while away a few hours next to the crackling fire in the salon attached to the main dining room. Harking back to an age of luxurious simplicity, the chef has designed an all-day menu that includes old British staples like mince and potatoes, yet also a high tea, with tasty morsels such as pork pie with Piccalilli. The afternoon tea carries the same traditional values, with ham sandwiches, a good scone and a small selection of cakes. If you get carried away in the spirit of the place, there are lovely rooms in the adjoining hotel to roll into.

69 - 71 Dean Street, Soho, W1D 3SE • www.deanstreettownhouse.com • 020 7434 1775

Stephen Tonkin's Gloucester Old Spot Sausage Roll

Serves 10

1kg Gloucester Old Spot sausage meat

175g Keens cheddar cheese, grated

30g sage, lightly chopped

500g pack of puff pastry

Salt

Pepper

Egg yolk, beaten

Mix all the sausage filling ingredients together (i.e. apart from puff pastry and egg yolk) and season well with the salt and pepper.

Chill and roll into a sausage about 3-4cm wide.

Roll out the puff pastry to 10mm thick.

Place the sausage in the centre then fold over each side of the pastry and wrap the sausage mix in the puff pastry.

Chill for a couple of minutes or until ready to cook.

Brush with beaten egg yolk evenly and sprinkle a little sea salt on top.

Cut to form sausage rolls about 10cm long and place on a baking tray.

Cook at 180°C for 16 minutes.

Serve with tomato ketchup and HP Sauce.

FORTNUM & MASON

With its iconic green and gold colouring, cuckoo clock from which miniature figures of Mr Fortnum and Mr Mason appear every fifteen minutes, and its liveried doormen, this is perhaps one of the most iconic institutions in which to take tea in London. What began in 1707 as a supplier of candles to the Royal Household has grown into a world-famous institution that is unashamedly traditional. It is well worth threading your way through the throngs of tourists and heading for the St. James's Restaurant designed to reflect the grace of the Georgian era. Afternoon tea begins with an interesting array of sandwiches, which vary with the seasons but may include finger sandwiches of coronation chicken with fresh mango and chilli, rolls with rare breed hens egg and mustard and cress, and oak smoked salmon with lemon butter on blinis. Scones come with an array of Fortnum & Mason jams including wild blueberry, lemon curd and apricot. These are followed by an array of tempting miniature cakes and tarts. As an accompaniment there is a choice of 70 blends or single-estate teas from Fortnum's own collection. Menus change with the seasons and to tie in with London events such as art exhibitions at the neighbouring Royal Academy, and Wimbledon. Afternoon tea can also be taken in The Fountain, The Gallery or The Parlour, but the St. James's Restaurant is the place for a traditional tea on a special occasion.

181 Piccadilly, W1A 1ER · www.fortnumandmason.com · 0845 300 1707

LA FROMAGERIE

L a Fromagerie started life in a garden shed in Highgate. It was the love of a mountain cheese called Beaufort Chalet d'Alpage that pushed the business forward. Once on the trail of cheesemakers who followed the path of producing traditional regional cheeses using milk from their own herd it naturally led to owner Patricia Michelson finding other foods such as meats, wines, and other ingredients and confectionery to showcase in the business.

Now the Moxon Street shop is packed with artisanal delights from purple carrots to almond milk and rose syrup, all overflowing in rustic baskets piled high on the shelves. It is almost impossible to leave without some edible delight, carried in one of the jaunty string bags they have for sale. Take tea on the large communal candlelit table surrounded by shelves of stacked wine and an antique clock. The main table seats 16, and there are a few more dotted around.

Tea time treats coming up from the kitchen could be the dark chocolate Brownies, flourless Chocolate Cake, or Orange and Almond Cake with a lovely spicy orange syrup; alongside try the Sri Lankan Estate Teas from Robert Wilson, a scented Violet tea, or the wonderful Piantagioni coffee from Tuscany. For serious indulgence, try their super rich Valrhona hot chocolate, or for an afternoon pick-me-up, their own recipe double espresso, laced with liqueur de noix.

2-6 Moxon Street, Marylebone, W1U 4EW · www.lafromagerie.co.uk · 020 7935 0341

Dark Chocolate Pecan Nut Brownies

Makes 12

500g Valrhona 70% dark
Gianduja chocolate,
broken into small pieces

500g unsalted Charente-
Poitou Butter

12 large free-range organic eggs

750g caster sugar

125g plain flour

125g Valrhona 100% cocoa powder

125g pecan nuts

"The secret to brownies is to use the best chocolate, butter and cocoa powder. The choice of nuts is up to you but I like the sweet nuttiness of pecans, but often use lightly toasted walnuts or hazelnuts.
To help you in the preparation, the chocolate, butter and eggs should all be at room temperature. As with all baking it is lightness of touch and thoroughness of mixing that will give the best results."

Preheat oven to 175°C.

Line a 23-25cm baking tin with parchment – even if it is non-stick as this will help you unmould – and leave a 5cm overhang all round as the brownies rise in the oven and then deflate once out and cool. Lightly grease the parchment with butter.

Have a saucepan with boiling water on a medium-low heat and place a mixing bowl on top – but the water should not touch the bowl. Melt the butter a little and then add the chocolate broken into small pieces and stir with a spatula until smooth.

Remove from the heat and with a large balloon whisk beat in the sugar until it is well mixed in. (You could use a kitchen aid or electric whisk if preferred).

Beat the eggs in a separate bowl and pour in a thin ribbon into the chocolate mixture while beating with a large balloon whisk. (You may prefer to pour the egg mixture into a jug to do this). You can stop from time to time to make sure the egg and chocolate are mixing well together.

Combine the flour and cocoa powder and place them in a fine-mesh sieve to sift into the chocolate/egg mixture. Fold in and then beat well for at least 3 minutes (You may want to do this in a mixer or use a hand-held electric blender). The mixture must be smooth and glossy without any grainy bits – you can check this by lifting the mixture up with the whisk to see how it pours back into the bowl.

Break up the pecans into large pieces and fold into the chocolate/egg/flour mixture with a wooden spoon.

Once all amalgamated pour into the baking tray, gently shake the tray to evenly spread the mixture and bake on the middle shelf of the oven for around 30-35 minutes or until the centre is just set – it can be soft and a little runny – but don't overcook as the brownies will still be 'cooking' even when they come out of the oven to rest and get to room temperature.

Once cooled down, turn the tin upside down and peel back the parchment.

Cut the brownies into 12 pieces, dust with a little cocoa powder and enjoy with tea or coffee, or even hot chocolate!

GALLERY MESS
SAATCHI GALLERY

I t might not be instantly recognisable as an officers' mess. A neon sign flashes with the word Buddha, an oversized shoe sculpture lies against a wall and bathroom walls are made of soap. Terence Koh's installation *Big White Cock* and Dan Attoe's *Forgiveness*, which depicts a nude woman on all fours with her mouth open and stars emitting from her backside, may well make the genteel folk of Chelsea blush into their macchiatos. Yet when Charles Saatchi opened his vast free-entry contemporary art gallery, it was never going to be boring. Art lovers can ponder the meaning of art and life over a cappuccino in the vaulted café that once housed the officers' mess in its former incarnation as a military barracks and training academy. Charles Saatchi converted the iconic 1801 listed building in 2008, and it has since held exhibitions from *Indian Art Today* to *Abstract America*. The café feels like a haven from the bustle of Duke of York Square and the King's Road, and with blossom resplendent with fairy lights, it has an almost arcadian air. Teas are simple – a selection of sandwiches, and warm scones with clotted cream and jam, accompanied by a range of different teas, from mint to chamomile and Earl Grey. There is also a Prosecco tea on offer, which comes with a glass of Brut di Pino Nero Rosé VS, Ruggeri.

If absorbing all this is enough to inspire you to want some of the action for yourself, much of the art on the walls is for sale, selected from web showcase Saatchi Online. During the summer the tables outside make a sunny vantage point from which to watch Chelsea life drift by.

Duke of York's HQ King's Road, Chelsea, SW3 4SQ · www.saatchi-gallery.co.uk · 020 7730 8135

GALLERY MESS
Apple & Quince Pie

Serves 4

1 quince

3 apples

125g sugar

Pinch of cinnamon

1 vanilla pod

1 lemon, juiced

250g flour

85g sugar

170g butter

Peel and dice the apples and quince.

Place them in a small saucepan with the vanilla pod, cinnamon and lemon juice.

Put on a low heat and cook for 10-12 minutes until they are almost soft. Then place into serving dish.

Preheat the oven to 200°C.

To make the shortbread topping, cream the butter and sugar together in a mixing bowl, then add the flour.

Chill the dough and roll out to 0.5cm thick. Cut a disc to fit the top of the serving dish then bake on a baking tray for 20-25 minutes or until the shortbread is golden in colour.

When it is ready to serve, place the shortbread on top of the apple and quince pie mixture and reheat in an oven for 10 minutes or until suitably hot.

Serve with crème anglaise for a delicious teatime treat.

GROSVENOR HOUSE

Overlooking Hyde Park, Grosvenor House offers one of the most diverse selections of cream teas in London. Although the hotel is not as much of a draw as some of its glitzy Park Lane neighbours, the Park Room is a destination for many scone lovers. Served in the charming mint green and pink room afternoon tea here takes its inspiration from Anna, 7th Duchess of Bedford, who supposedly asked for a light meal between lunch and dinner whilst visiting the 5th Duke of Rutland at Belvoir Castle in the mid 1800s, thus inventing the idea of afternoon tea. Anna's Tea at Grosvenor House includes buttermilk scones, sandwiches with well-sourced products such as Hebridean smoked salmon, and a selection of delicious pastries. However, here, children are also looked after and can enjoy a Grover's tea, named after the hotel's canine mascot. This includes bite-size cakes, ice cream, elderflower cordial and a Grover toy to take home. There is also a Hendricks tea which includes a Hendrick's gin Martini, for those who need a little afternoon pick-me-up, and Tate and Lyle teas with lashings of golden syrup. An interesting addition is that gluten free teas are also offered. There is a pianist playing in the corner, and a central stand displays the many cakes on offer. These include opera gâteau, Victoria sponge and fresh raspberry tart. Interesting loose-teas include flowering jasmine and lily tea, and Chinese Puerh tea.

Park Lane, Mayfair, W1K 7TN · www.marriott.co.uk · 020 7499 6363

Scones

Serves 10

312g soft flour

Pinch of salt

9g baking powder

52g butter

112g caster sugar

208g whipping cream

½ medium orange (zested)

40g sultanas

Egg for egg wash

Mix all the dry ingredients with the soft butter like a crumble and mix well.

Add the whipping cream and mix to a nice dough.

Cover and place the mixture in the fridge to rest for 30 minutes.

Remove from the fridge and roll out the dough to approximately 2-2.5cm thick.

Cut into 10 triangles, place on a baking sheet and egg wash.

Allow the scones to rest at room temperature for 15-20 minutes.

Bake at 160°C for 18 minutes.

HIX

SELFRIDGES

Strategically situated above the handbag floor in the megalithic temple to designer wares that is Selfridges, Hix is a place where harassed shoppers can watch as teenagers crowd around the latest calfskin delight below, discuss the sensibility of blowing the mortgage on a beautifully cut tank top, or merely a lovely place to come and escape the awfulness of Oxford Street. Mark Hix is deeply entrenched in the British tradition and here there are buttery crumpets, waffles and scones with cream and jam. However, he is best known for his fish and seafood creations, and a truly decadent afternoon can be spent trying caviar treats including those made with their fully sustainable Latvian caviar – washed down with a glass of Champagne from one of the small independent producers Hix supports. For serious appetites the lobster thermidor is a treat. It may be an indulgence, but so is the £4000 charged for the handbags on sale below. Oxford Street is a headache at the best of times, and this well-placed restaurant makes it a little bit more bearable. As in all his restaurants, Mark Hix also showcases his collection of art by his drinking pals including Tracey Emin, Mat Collishaw and Gary Webb. Those slimming for a Roland Mouret frock can join the numerous other clients who prefer a purely liquid afternoon propped up against the pewter Champagne and crustacean bar.

400 Oxford Street, Marylebone, W1A 1AB · www.hixatselfridges.co.uk · 020 7499 5400

THE HUMMINGBIRD BAKERY

Ever since the Sex in the City girls showed what scoffing copious cupcakes could do for the figure – keep you svelte and able to slip into the latest sample size couture piece – the cupcake craze has refused to die. Now a firm fixture at weddings and fashion events, it proves that if you dress something beautifully, not even fashionistas care about the calories. Which is lucky as these decadent offerings are slathered in highly addictive cream cheese toppings – that for some, are the main event. At the forefront from the start of the craze is the Hummingbird Bakery, which was started by Tarek Malouf in 2004 in Portobello Road. With cafés and shops in Notting Hill, Soho, South Kensington and Spitalfields, each branch makes the calorie-laden treats fresh in their kitchen daily. There are seasonal specialities such as gingerbread or eggnog for Christmas. Their bestseller is still the moreish red velvet cupcake, which tastes as good as it looks. The red vanilla sponge has a hint of chocolate and is topped with a thick layer of cream cheese frosting. This also comes as one of their range of cakes – which includes vanilla sponge, chocolate devil and carrot which are great for lazy chefs who want to impress their dinner party guests. For another slice of Americana, there are also pies on offer, including pumpkin, Mississippi mud or key lime, not to mention devilish brownies and whoopie pies – the latest craze to cross the pond.

155a Wardour Street, Soho, W1F 8WG · www.hummingbirdbakery.com · 020 7851 1795

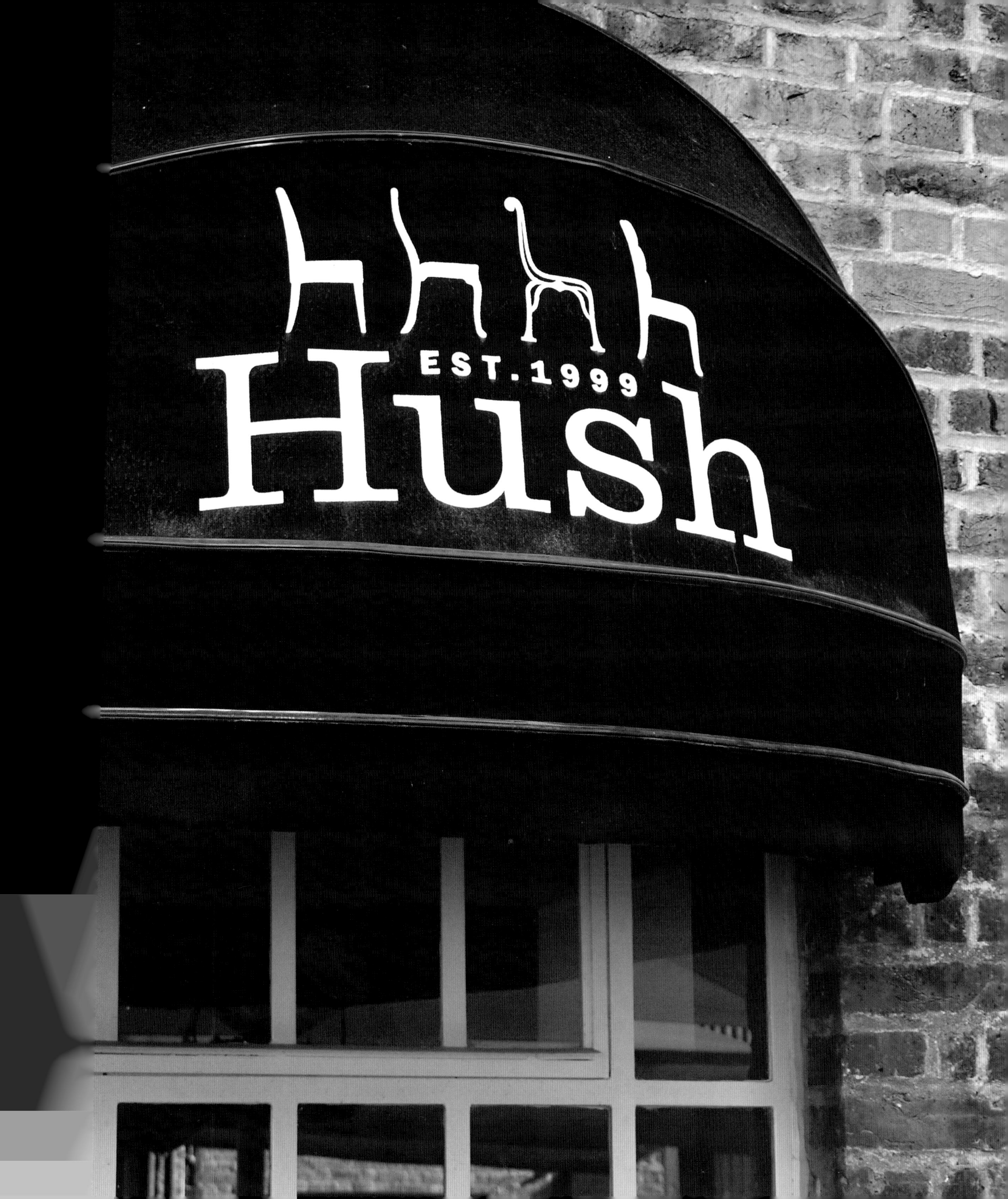
EST. 1999
Hush

HUSH

If you slip into the relative calm of Lancashire Court from busy New Bond Street during shopping hours, you feel the excitement of entering a hidden oasis while the world shops around you. Entering from a deserted New Bond Street in the evening, the area can be more reminiscent of Gin Lane – with its well refreshed crowds of after work drinkers. Tucked away in a hidden courtyard is the brasserie cum bar cum screening venue, Hush.

At afternoon tea, you can feel at something of a crossroads. The shops are still open, but on a winter's night the dark is setting in. So while the scones and macaroons of the Classic Cream Tea (served with or without a Hendrick's gin cocktail) or a Mayfair Tea will be just fine, it seems a shame not to get into the spirit of the place and opt for the Hendrick's High tea, named after the quirky small batch gin distilled using a combination of traditional stills and served from distinctive apothecary-style brown bottles.

You can bridge the tea / early evening drink divide perfectly with a "Lady Gray", a Hendrick's molecular cocktail with Earl Grey tea foam, and you'll soon find yourself ordering more (how about a Wild Orchid Jam Martini with Hendrick's gin, blackberry jam, sake and elderflower cordial), and, if it's a Saturday evening you could soon be enjoying one of the screenings in the courtyard at the front of Hush. Where did the time go? Hush, and enjoy yourself.

8 Lancashire Court, Brook Street, Mayfair, W1S 1EY · www.hush.co.uk · 020 7659 1500

KONDITOR & COOK
THE GHERKIN

The Queen of Hearts she made some tarts, all on a summer's day,
The Knave of Hearts he stole the tarts and took them clean away.
The King of Hearts called for the tarts and beat the Knave full sore
The Knave of Hearts brought back the tarts and vowed he'd steal no more.

He didn't need to steal any more – he would bake his own. On the site of the old Queen of Hearts bakery in Waterloo, Gerhard Jenne, the founder of Konditor & Cook, opened his first branch in 1993 and soon established himself not so much as a knave, more as the King of the baking revival in London.

Gerhard was trained in Munich as a "Konditor" or pâtisserie chef, and focuses very much on natural ingredients, free-range eggs and contemporary cake decorating techniques. His range of brownies, including the Fudgepacker quickly achieved a reputation as some of the best in London. Perhaps the most popular of the cakes available in various sizes includes the Curly Wurly, a chocolate sponge with real vanilla bean frosting.

But there's a lot more at Konditor & Cook than brownies and sponges. There are the "Original Magic Cakes", hand-decorated lemon cakes, and a number of classics (bakewell slice, millionaire's shortbread, and many more) plus tartlets and slab cakes and all sorts of treats for breakfast.

Konditor has now expanded beyond the original Waterloo shop to a number of branches in the West End, South Bank and City. Each has its own charm and style, but the baking is excellent whichever branch you choose.

30 St Mary Axe, The City, EC3A 8BF · www.konditorandcook.com · 0844 854 9369

Gingerbread Dough*

Makes 12-16

150g soft brown sugar

4 tbs golden syrup

2 tbs black treacle

1 tbs cinnamon

1 tbs ground ginger

1 pinch ground cloves

1 grated orange zest

2 tbs water

175g salted butter, cubed

1 tsp bicarbonate soda

400g plain flour, sifted

In a small pan combine sugar, syrup, treacle, spices and orange zest with 2 tbs water. Bring to the boil while stirring.

Remove from heat and stir in the butter until melted; then add the bicarbonate of soda.

Next stir in the flour while the mixture is still warm.
Remove the dough from the pan, wrap and chill for 1 hour or up to 1 week.

To bake, roll out the dough on a lightly floured surface to 4-5mm thickness.

Cut out approximately 12-16 shapes with cookie cutters and place well apart on a baking tray lined with baking parchment.

Cook in a preheated oven at 180°C for approximately 15 minutes.

Remove from the oven and leave to cool on the tray.

Once cool, they are ready to be eaten or decorated.

*At Christmas this is a very handy recipe. You can use it to create Christmas tree decorations, name tags for a festive table, or fulfil your dream of being an architect and build your own grand design gingerbread house.
This recipe is reliable and makes a malleable dough, easy for children to use too.

LADURÉE

HARRODS

What started as a bakery at 16 rue Royale in Paris in 1862, has morphed into the most famous macaroon tearoom in the world. In 2005 a branch opened in Harrods. The room is decked out in huge slabs of marble with rococo touches, the shelves stacked full of temptations to take home. There is also an outdoor café, perfect on a sunny day, in this relatively quiet corner of Knightsbridge. Ladurée is best known for its delicate almond macaroons, flavoured with coffee, pistachio or a zingy lemon; yet there are also more adventurous ones to try including blackcurrant and violet, salted caramel, and rose and ginger. There is also a selection of club sandwiches, and pâtisserie. Some say that you are better off sticking to what it does best and focus on the macaroons but they also serve a fine afternoon tea consisting of finger sandwiches, mini viennoiseries and pastries. Their own brand tea selections include Lapsang Souchong, a delicately smoked China tea, Thé au Caramel, which is a black Ceylon tea scented with caramel and flowers, and Oolong, a China tea scented with orange blossom.

Ladurée provides an antidote to what is either one of the most wonderful or most harrowing shopping experiences in the world.

87–135 Brompton Road, Knightsbridge, SW1X 7XL · www.harrods.com · 020 3155 0111

Chocolate French Macaroons

Makes 50

Chocolate ganache
(make 2 hours before the biscuit)

325g bitter chocolate,
finely chopped
300g single cream
75g butter

Bring the cream to the boil and add the chocolate.

With the mixture no hotter than 60°C, add the butter.

Leave to cool to room temperature; the ganache should remain soft.

Chocolate macaroon biscuits

275g icing sugar
140g ground almonds
25g cocoa powder
4 egg whites (120g)
20g caster sugar

In a food processor bowl, combine the almonds, icing sugar and cocoa powder to obtain a fine powder. Sieve.

Beat the egg whites to stiff peaks, adding the sugar while still beating.

Next, fold in the almond and cocoa mixture quickly but gently (to mix well, place the spoon in the middle of the bowl, move to the side and come back to the centre while turning the bowl regularly) until you obtain a smooth, even, slightly runny consistency.

Using a piping bag (1cm diameter), pipe small macaroons onto baking parchment.

Leave to rest for 20 minutes before placing the macaroons in the oven to lightly crisp up.

Bake for 10 to 12 minutes on a sturdy baking tray in an oven preheated to 180°C.

Remove the tray from the oven and, using a glass, pour a small amount of water between the tray and the paper (lift the paper gradually corner by corner). The moisture and steam from the water on the hot tray will make it easier to remove the macaroons from the paper when cool.

Spread a layer of ganache (3-4mm) on each biscuit and stick the macaroons together in pairs (or leave them plain by sticking them together as soon as you have moistened the tray).

Tips

For various reasons, the macaroons may crack on the underside. This may be due to the ingredients, the oven or your mixing method. Whatever the reason, don't give up! Cracked or not, they will taste just as delicious. With experience, they will be smooth.

Leave the finished macaroons to set for 24 hours in the fridge. During this time, the different ingredients will come together to enhance and refine the taste and texture of the macaroons.

For plain or jam macaroons, replace the cocoa powder with ground almonds.

Filling suggestions

Mix 500g of low-sugar jam (60% fruit and 40% sugar maximum) with 75g of ground almonds. Try to use jams made from tangy fruit (raspberry, apricot, redcurrant or blackcurrant) with a stronger flavour.

Macaroons can also be garnished with homemade lemon cream, a cream made from flavoured butter, or even soft caramel.

THE LANGHAM

S ituated off the bustle of Regent Street, this was allegedly the first hotel to serve afternoon tea, in 1865, and counts Sir Arthur Conan Doyle amongst its historic tea-taking clientèle. The Palm Court, situated immediately in front of the main entrance has huge vases of flowers, Holbein blue low velvet stools, and mirrored tables and ceiling to make up for the lack of natural light.

Tea is a traditional affair up to a point, with a pianist who plays daily on a royal blue grand piano. Tea sommelier Alex Probyn has chosen a range of over 30 teas, including two house blends – The Langham and The Palm Court. The traditional afternoon tea offers an interesting selection of finger sandwiches including crayfish with fennel and crème fraîche, and seasonal offerings such as smoked duck with celeriac and crispy shallots during winter. For a slightly more off the wall approach, jeweller Stephen Webster's Bijoux Afternoon Tea is inspired by his latest jewellery collections. As well as some interesting sandwiches, including lobster with piquillo peppers and flying fish roe, the scones have an alcoholic touch with the raisins soaked in Louis Roederer Champagne. His intricate cakes refer to the jeweller's collections and include poison apple, dagger dome and an armadillo ring.

1c Portland Place, Marylebone, W1B 1JA · www.london.langhamhotels.co.uk · 020 7636 1000

LONDON REVIEW BOOKSHOP

This is perfect for bibliophiles who want to imbibe a good cuppa while contemplating the latest neo-Kantian arguments, browse a magazine or book bought from the well-stocked shop over a dainty cake or sandwich, or just relax in the quiet room. The tea room – connected to the shop by a passage in the history section – is light, airy and unassuming, but that should not deter you from the tasty cakes on offer. These can include pistachio and rose, light, fluffy cupcakes, lemon tarts or green cardamom and white chocolate brownies. You will also notice some North African influences in the food, the region being a favourite culinary inspiration for the Manager, Terry Glover. The teashop is a lovely place in which you can unashamedly indulge your academic fantasies over a freshly made ciabatta sandwich or slice of quiche. Books in the shop are arranged by subject matter ranging from Mythology and Folklore to Performance Studies as well as all the latest novels. They take the choice of tea particularly seriously at the café including a range of Oolongs – and they serve great coffee too. This peaceful spot is located a stone's throw away from the British Museum so is the place for the academically inclined for whom a good book and decent cup of tea is more important than liveried waiters and tinkly pianos.

14 Bury Place, Holborn, WC1A 2JL • www.lrbshop.co.uk • 020 7269 9045

MAISON BERTAUX

Beloved of local thespians and Soho eccentrics, this higgledy-piggledy blue-and-white fronted café is full of creative waifs and strays, who flock to sisters Michelle and Tania Wade's pâtisserie to indulge themselves. It is ramshackle and perhaps not the ideal place to take a somewhat particular elderly aunt, but if you want character and the Soho of old, this is your afternoon tea spot. The art is curated by Tania, with paintings from a wide range of regulars, including Mighty Boosh comedian and artist Noel Fielding. The café was established in 1871 by French communards when Soho had a far more fruity clientèle than today. However, you still might see some of the old colour if you sit long enough feasting on the delectable cakes made by Michelle. Up the creaky stairs is the gallery and slightly shambolic tearoom, which provides the perfect respite from the mayhem of Soho; or sit at one of the pavement tables and watch the world go by. Feast on their delightfully creamy Monts Blancs, strawberry tarts and pastries or sit and contemplate your next script over a cup of tea and a mustardy Dijon slice, surrounded by fairy lights and knick-knacks in one of the most atmospheric places in Soho. The service can be grouchy, but it's worth it for a bit of escapism from the more sterile modern Soho.

28 Greek Street, Soho, W1D 5DQ · www.maisonbertaux.com · 020 7437 6007

MAISON BERTAUX
Cheese Tarts

Makes 8-10

Shortcrust pastry
250g plain flour
125g cold butter, diced
3-4 tbs cold water

Sieve the flour into a bowl, mix with the pieces of butter using your fingertips until crumbly.

Add the water and mix all together.

Wrap and keep in the fridge for 30 minutes.

Roll out the pastry and line the tart cases with it.

Cheese tart mixture
100g butter
150g milk
270g Cheddar cheese
110g flour
Pinch salt
2 whole eggs

Melt the butter in a saucepan and add the flour gradually until it comes together.

Add the milk little by little, then add the grated cheese and keep stirring for 5 minutes.

Add the eggs one by one.

Put the mixture into a piping bag and fill the tart cases.

Bake in the oven for 15 minutes at 180°C.

THE MANDEVILLE HOTEL

Although the deVille Restaurant is not the most opulent room in which to take afternoon tea, it is fun, with its purple walls, neo-flock wallpaper, Venetian mask lights and perspex mirrors. Here, a stone's throw from South Molton Street and the irresistible charms of Marylebone High Street, tea is served between 3pm and 5.30pm during the week, and from 1pm at the weekend.

There is a choice of two teas. The doyenne of fashion design Zandra Rhodes has created her own Iconic Afternoon Tea featuring jewelled eclair fingers, macaroon buttons and lavender butterfly shortbread with a selection of sandwiches and classic scones. The accompanying teas include Whole Rose Bud, Jing Blackcurrant and Hibiscus, and Yellow Gold Oolong. The second choice is The Men's Afternoon Tea, which is a very masculine affair featuring roast sirloin sandwiches, potted shrimp, bourbon laced fruitcake, and, of course, the traditional scones, all washed down with a selection of teas, champagne or whiskies. Board games are available to add a competitive touch. There is also a gluten-free tea on offer with mocha chocolate cake, ginger cake and cookies.

Mandeville Place, Marylebone, W1U 2BE · www.mandeville.co.uk · 020 7935 5599

Pink Meringues
Granny's Lavender Shortbread

Makes 40

Pink meringues

125g egg whites
125g caster sugar
100g icing sugar
15g cornflour
Pink food colouring
Whipped cream (to serve)

Whisk the egg whites until they are stiff enough to make soft peaks.

Add a few drops of pink food colouring and then the caster sugar a little at a time whilst whisking until the mixture is able to form stiff peaks. This normally takes a little longer than you would expect.

Sieve the icing sugar and cornflour over the mixture and fold it in carefully by slicing it in with a large metal spoon. Avoid stirring the mixture too much or it will become soft.

When the icing sugar is completely integrated into the mixture, spoon it into a piping bag with a large starred nozzle and pipe 3cm by 3cm pyramids in a circular motion. Bake on greaseproof paper or a baking mat at 100°C for 2-3 hours.

Stick two meringues together back to back with whipped cream. If you're feeling fancy, you could give your pink meringues a light coating of pink edible lustre spray.

Granny's lavender shortbread

300g flour
50g cornflour
50g caster sugar
50g icing sugar
250g unsalted cold butter, cubed
25g dried lavender

Place all the ingredients in a food processor and blend until you have a crumbly, almost pastry consistency.

Cover a baking tray with greaseproof paper/baking mat and place the mixture on top.

Cover the dough with greaseproof paper and roll it out until it is about 4mm thick and bake for 15 minutes at 165°C.

Using a shape cutter cut out the shape 5 minutes after removing it from the oven.

Sprinkle a light coating of caster sugar on top.

MELT

Opened in 2004 in the heart of Notting Hill, it is virtually impossible to walk past this small chocolate shop without venturing in for a delicious mouthful to fuel a leisurely shop in the surrounding boutiques. Head Chocolatier Chika Watanabe – a former pastry chef at Claridge's and The Lanesborough – leads her team of Oompa Loompahs in the open kitchen behind the shop, where browsers can watch the mouthwatering creations take form. Perch at their bar and order one of their to-die-for hot chocolate shots which is worth crossing the capital for. Choose from one of the seven different single origin blocks – including Dark Venezuelan and Papua New Guinean. Each molten drink comes with its own tasting notes. To accompany this sinful shot choose some chocolates such as the banana passionfruit and coconut bonbon, the ginger and passion fruit cup, or the simple but unbelievably delicious milk chocolate truffle. A must visit if you do find yourself in Notting Hill – and perfect for those who want an afternoon sugar high without a full afternoon tea. The 90g single origin bars in their colourful packaging are lovely to take home. Melt also collaborates with other designers and chefs: try Mark Hix's Cider Apple Brandy chocolate or Sophie Conran's Earl Grey, ginger and cranberry. As Peanuts' creator Charles M. Schulz once said, "All you need is love, but a little bit of chocolate now and then doesn't hurt".

59 Ledbury Road, Notting Hill, W11 2AA · www.meltchocolates.com · 020 7727 5030

MO CAFÉ

Escape into the souk-like surrounds of the Mo Café, complete with berber rugs, brightly coloured latticed hanging lamps and dainty tables. For those who want the charm of the medina without having to negotiate the mules, mayhem and haggling, this is a stone's-throw from Regent Street and a welcome respite from the crowded streets. The tea fuses elements of British with North African, and chef Philippe Agnello has travelled the region picking up traditional Maghreb recipes along the way. Scones are served on a quirky cake stand consisting of different patterned plates accompanied by interesting sandwich offerings such as Moroccan chicken wrap, zaalouk and mechouia on toast and cheese briouats, followed by pastries dripping in honey and a moist fig macaroon. Teas come in a range of flavours including traditional mint, Hammam, which infuses green dates and red fruits, or a cardamom and citrus Fakir tea. These are all served in traditional brass teapots sourced by owner Mourad Mazouz.

The café also doubles as a bazaar with many of the surrounding textiles, lamps and artifacts for sale.

25 Heddon Street, Mayfair, W1B 4BH · www.momoresto.com · 020 7434 4040

Cinnamon & Date Scones with Strawberry & Fig Jam

Makes 1.5kg jam

Serves 40 using 350g jam

Strawberry & fig jam

500g strawberries

500g fig purée

600g caster sugar

16g pectin

40g lemon juice

Mix the sugar and pectin.

Put all the ingredients together in a saucepan and cook at 110°C until the jam thickens.

Cinnamon & date scones

900g flour t55

153g sugar

252g milk

180g eggs

153g chopped dates

60g baking powder

200g butter

10g cinnamon powder

Egg wash to glaze

Mix the flour, sugar, baking powder and butter.

Then add the milk and eggs and, finally, the dates. Do not over mix.

Roll out to the required thickness, then cut into desired shapes and glaze with egg wash.

Bake for 10 minutes at 160°C.

THE MODERN PANTRY

**W**hen you look across St John's Square in Clerkenwell on a winter afternoon, as darkness is beginning to set in, and see the tall windows of the Modern Pantry lit up, you know you're in for a welcome. But what you may not yet know is the culinary treat that awaits.

Anna Hansen, the owner and chef, originally trained under Fergus Henderson of neighbouring St John fame, but by 1994 she was working with Peter Gordon. As such she was very much part of the fusion revolution in the 1990s epitomised by the Sugar Club and Providores – she worked at both of these with Gordon.

Fusion is now firmly within the London mainstream, but Hansen still manages to conjure up surprises in her cooking while sticking to the mantra of good food. The first floor restaurant has the formal dining room, but for afternoon tea you'll be on the ground floor, and possibly on the long communal and sociable table. This is a place that manages to be mummy-friendly and informal yet not compromise on quality.

If you opt for the afternoon tea "with bubbles", you can start with the lychee, raspberry and rose Bellini to set you off before enjoying the award winning Newby tea (try the genmai cha) and Hansen's delicious sandwiches, sweet and savoury scones and cakes. While these are served on a cake stand, that's the only nod to tradition in this relaxed, but inventive place.

47-48 St John's Square, Clerkenwell, EC1V 4JJ · www.themodernpantry.co.uk · 020 7553 9210

Green Tea Scones with Gooseberry & Vanilla Compôte

Makes 12

Green tea scones

400g self-raising flour

2 tsp green tea powder

½ tsp baking powder

¼ tsp salt

80g caster sugar

80g unsalted butter, diced

300ml buttermilk or whole milk

A little extra milk for brushing

Granulated or demerara sugar
for sprinkling

Gooseberry & vanilla compôte

1 vanilla pod

500g gooseberries

100g white sugar

A squeeze of lemon juice

First make the compôte. Slit the vanilla pod open lengthwise and scrape out the seeds.

Put the pod and seeds in a pan with gooseberries, sugar and lemon juice.

Bring to the boil, then cover the pan, reduce the heat to low and simmer for 5 minutes or so, until the gooseberries are just tender but mostly still hold their shape.

Remove from the heat and leave to cool completely before serving.

For the scones, sift the flour, green tea powder, baking powder and salt into a food processor.

Add the sugar and butter and pulse until the mixture resembles fine crumbs. Tip into a bowl, then add the buttermilk or milk and mix to form a dough, being careful not to over work.

Lightly dust a work surface with flour, turn the dough out onto to it and flatten to about 2.5cm thick.

Cut into 12 squares with a knife, or use a pastry cutter if you prefer, and transfer to a baking sheet.

Brush with milk, sprinkle over some sugar and place in an oven preheated to 220°C.

Bake for 10-12 minutes, until golden brown.

NATIONAL PORTRAIT GALLERY

You would be forgiven for thinking that in a restaurant with a view as good as the National Portrait Gallery's, the food would play a secondary role – especially when it is attached to the world's largest collection of portraits. However, Swedish head chef Katarina Todosijevic has ensured that the food is very much at the centre of the experience, whether at lunch, afternoon tea, or dinner.

With a wall of glass overlooking Trafalgar Square, you are guaranteed a view, even if your table is located on the back wall of the restaurant. Once you have found the right lift to the restaurant (it's in the Ondaatje Wing), you can enjoy views of Big Ben, the Houses of Parliament, the London Eye, and, of course, the events and sculptures of Trafalgar Square. Afternoon tea is served in two sittings, with a well-executed, if traditional set menu that can include rosé champagne and smoked salmon sandwiches if you choose the Champagne Afternoon Tea. You can also order items individually. The cake selection changes but recently included a delicious cranberry shortbread and a St Clement's crème brûlée.

Another plus is that you can often get a table as a walk-in – and if not, there are few more interesting places to while away the few minutes you may have to wait.

St Martin's Place, Trafalgar Square, WC2H 0HE · www.npg.org.uk · 020 7312 2490

NUMBER SIXTEEN

Located in an elegant townhouse in a leafy residential street this mid-Victorian 42-bedroom hotel is a welcome retreat from the madness of the local museums and galleries. Tea is served all day and can be taken in any of the communal areas. During the summer, the most glorious is the tree-lined garden. Find a quiet corner and sip on teas ranging from Earl Grey to Jasmine Silver Tip. During the winter the Drawing Room provides a colourful escape from the gloom – bold pink floor to ceiling curtains, pink chaises longues and bright butterfly art by Allyson Reynolds is the cheeriest environment in which to enjoy afternoon tea. There is also a library, which has more of a club feel with a three-dimensional work by Eric Race depicting three men fishing for stars. The tea includes ham and mustard, and cucumber and balsamic sandwiches, pineapple, banana and walnut cake, and a fruit tartlet. A simple cream tea is available at a very reasonable price which is simply scones and tea. A fruit tea is a guilt-free option. Feast on caramelised banana, and mango and pineapple salad with cracked pepper, among other treats. Speciality teas include Green Jasmine Flower Blossom and Rooibos. If you are in the residential area of South Kensington this is a great place for tea.

16 Sumner Place, South Kensington, SW7 3EG · www.firmdale.com · 020 7589 5232

179

ONE ALDWYCH

I t would be hard to find a floral display as magnificent as the one that greets you in the huge Lobby Bar of this five-star hotel. Originally opened in 1907 and designed by Ritz architects Charles Mewes and Arthur Davies, its original incarnation was as the newspaper offices of *The Morning Post* newspaper. Today, huge urns perched high on perspex plinths divide the light airy room with its magnificent floor-to-ceiling windows and towering columns. Depending on the time of day it is packed with businessmen cutting deals over morning coffee or theatregoers downing glasses of Prosecco before the curtain goes up. However, the afternoon lull is the best time to appreciate this light-flooded atrium with its contemporary sculptures. If you are visiting the theatre, it is ideally situated. The offerings are classic and unfussy – chicken and Colman mayonnaise or smoked salmon and horseradish sandwiches. Indulge in the Welsh Rarebit with tomato before tucking into the cake selection, which includes apple trifle, carrot cake and Battenberg. Teas from the Covent Garden Tea Palace include Darjeeling First Flush, Imperial Ceylon and White Monkey Green Tea. The space starts to fill up around 5pm – when an enthusiastic after-work crowd descends on the long black bar at the back of the room.

1 Aldwych, Covent Garden, WC2B 4BZ · www.onealdwych.com · 020 7300 1000

Quail Scotch Eggs with Gribiche Sauce

Serves 4

Scotch eggs

4 quail eggs
150g pork sausage meat
1 small onion, finely chopped
4 sage leaves, finely chopped
½ egg, beaten
15g breadcrumbs
100g plain flour
1 egg, whisked
Vegetable oil for frying

Gribiche sauce

100g mayonnaise
1 dessert spoon gherkins,
finely chopped
1 dessert spoon capers,
finely chopped
1 dessert spoon chopped parsley
1 dessert spoon chopped tarragon
1 dessert spoon chopped shallots
1 egg, hard boiled, with yolk and
white chopped separately
½ lemon, juiced

Plunge the quail eggs into boiling water (straight from the fridge) and leave them in the water for 2 minutes 20 seconds.

Remove from the pan and drop immediately into iced water. After 3 minutes, remove and shell the eggs.

Mix the sausage meat, onion, sage, egg and breadcrumbs to make a farce and season.

Divide this mixture into 4 and mould around the quail eggs rolling into an egg shape.

Leave to set in the fridge for 1 hour and then roll through flour, whisked egg and breadcrumbs.

Deep fry in the oil at 180°C for 3 minutes 30 seconds.

To make the sauce, gently fold all the other ingredients into the mayonnaise and season with salt and pepper.

Cut the quail eggs in half and sprinkle with pepper and rock salt. Serve with the gribiche sauce.

OTTOLENGHI

With its piles of featherlight meringues, slabs of gooey chocolate brownies, and wonderfully fresh platters of salads, it is hard to walk by any of the four stores in Notting Hill, Belgravia, Islington and Kensington without indulging. What started as mainly a shop, has now become a stopping point for well-heeled foodies, local mothers and a health conscious workforce looking to stock up on take home sugary delights and delicious salads packed with fashionable ingredients such as pomegranate seeds and quinoa. There is no afternoon tea as such, however the portions are huge and a couple of these shared between friends is more than enough. Try their legendary flourless chocolate cake or mini lemon meringue pies. The original shop in Notting Hill only seats ten but Islington takes bookings and seats 50, making it a good place for a group. Opened in 2002 by Yotam Ottolenghi, who came to London to study Cordon Bleu, rather like Daylesford, his shops have become less retail outlets and more a lifestyle in themselves – his cookbooks are ubiquitous in the capital's kitchens. Predictably for such chic neighbourhoods, popping into the distinctive red and white shops for a salad and slice of cake can be eye-wateringly expensive.

287 Upper Street, Islington, N1 2TZ · www.ottolenghi.co.uk · 020 7288 1454

Pear & Amaretto Crumble Cake

Serves 4-6

Melted butter for greasing the tins

100g (peeled weight) Bramley apple, peeled and cut into 1.5cm dice (about ½ apple)

150g (peeled weight) pear, peeled and cut into 1.5cm dice (about 1 pear)

30g toasted walnuts, roughly chopped

Grated zest of 1 lemon

2 tbsp Amaretto liqueur

210g plain flour

¾ tsp baking powder

¾ tsp ground cinnamon

1/3 tsp ground cloves

45g ground almonds

3 free-range eggs

180ml sunflower oil

230g caster sugar

1/3 tsp salt

120g crumble mixture (see below)

Crumble

300g plain four

100g caster sugar

200g cold unsalted butter cut into small cubes

Preheat the oven to 170°C. Grease 2 small (500g) loaf tins with melted butter and line the base and sides with baking parchment.

Mix the chopped apple and pear with the walnuts, lemon zest and Amaretto liqueur. In a separate bowl, sift together the flour, baking powder, cinnamon and cloves. Add the ground almonds.

Separate 2 of the eggs, keeping the whites separate while mixing the yolks with the third egg. Using an electric mixer, beat together the oil and sugar for about a minute (this can also be done by hand, mixing briskly with a spatula). On a low speed, slowly add the yolk and egg mix. Quickly add the sifted dry ingredients, followed by the fruit mix. Stop the machine as soon as everything is incorporated.

Whisk the egg whites with the salt until they form firm peaks, then gently fold them into the cake mix, using a spatula or metal spoon. Again, be careful not to over mix. Streaks of white in the mixture are okay.

Divide the cake mix between the tins and scatter the crumble on top. Bake for 40-45 minutes, until a skewer inserted in the centre comes out clean. (It might take a bit longer, depending on the moisture content of the fruit). If the cakes start going dark before the centre is cooked, cover them with foil.

Remove from the oven and leave to cool, then remove the cakes from the tins.

Put the flour, sugar and butter in a bowl and mix with your hands or an electric mixer fitted with the beater attachment to work it to a uniform breadcrumb consistency. Make sure there are no lumps of butter left. If using a mixer, watch it carefully. Within a few seconds, a crumble can turn into cookie dough. (If this unpleasant scenario happens, roll it out thinly, cut out cookies, bake them and half dip in melted chocolate).

Transfer the crumble to a plastic container. It will keep in the fridge for up to 5 days, or for ages in the freezer.

PEGGY PORSCHEN

This pink and cream escape located on the corner of Belgravia's chic Elizabeth and Ebury Streets is rather like attending a friend's tea party. Sit at one of the round metal tables, surrounded by the local blonde Tod's wearing brigade who frequent this place to nibble on delicate cupcakes and sup bespoke teas. German born Peggy Porschen, who came to London in 1998 to study at the Cordon Bleu cookery school, opened the doors to her café in 2010 after a successful career as a bespoke cakemaker and author of three books on the subject. Cake maker to the stars, she has catered for the likes of Madonna, Gwyneth Paltrow and Elton John. As well as a bespoke cakemaking service and an academy where you can learn the art of cakemaking (courses include cupcake and cookie making), the store sells a select range of sugary delights. Apart from her award winning range of cupcakes including Black Forest gâteau and banoffee pie, the carrot cake is to die for and the cookies light and crumbly. Teas have been specially blended inspired by flavours found in her kitchen. A selection of these expensive but beautifully presented cakes can be bought to take home; but budding domestic goddesses can buy one of the cake-making kits or accessories on offer if they prefer. There are also teas and vintage crockery for sale.

16 Ebury Street, Chelsea, SW1W 9QQ · www.peggyporschen.com · 020 7730 1316

Apple Strudel Cupcakes

Makes 20-24

Calvados & cinnamon frosting

200g full-fat cream cheese at room temperature
200g unsalted butter, softened
500g icing sugar, sifted
½ tsp ground cinnamon
30ml Calvados

Place the cream cheese into a mixing bowl and beat gently until smooth and creamy.

Place the butter and the icing sugar into a separate bowl and cream together until very pale and fluffy.

Add the cream cheese, a little at a time, to the butter mixture and mix at medium speed until the frosting is combined.

Add the cinnamon and Calvados. Chill until set.

Cake mix

65g sultanas
25ml Calvados
3 medium eggs
Grated zest of 1 lemon
250g caster sugar
115ml vegetable oil
80g hazelnuts, chopped and toasted / plus extra for decoration (optional)
450g Bramley apples, finely chopped
280g self-raising flour
35g ground hazelnuts
1¼ tsp ground cinnamon
½ tsp ground cloves
½ tsp ground nutmeg
Pinch of ground ginger. Pinch of salt

Soak the sultanas with the Calvados, ideally several days in advance.

Pre-heat the oven to 160°C.

Line the muffin baking trays with the cup cake liners.

Place the sugar, the oil and the lemon zest into a mixing bowl and beat until smooth.

Lightly beat the eggs and add gradually to the mixture while beating.

Add the sultanas, the chopped hazelnuts and apples, and mix together.

Sift the remaining dry ingredients together and mix gently until combined.

Put the mixture into the cup cake liners up to about ¾ full.

Bake for about 20 to 25 minutes or until the cakes are golden brown and the tops spring back to the touch. If inserting a knife or skewer it should come out just clean.

Syrup

50ml water
50ml lemon juice
150g caster sugar
50ml Calvados

While the cupcakes are baking, place the sugar, the lemon juice and the water into a saucepan and bring to the boil. Cook until the sugar has dissolved and set aside to cool down.

Once cool, add the Calvados.

Brush the syrup over the cupcakes while they are still warm and let them cool completely.

Special equipment

2 muffin trays with 12 wells each
24 cup cake liners

To serve

Either pipe the frosting on top of the cup cakes with a piping bag or spread it over with a palette knife. To garnish sprinkle a few chopped and toasted hazelnuts over the top.

Enjoy at room temperature. The cupcakes have a shelf-life of about 3 days if stored in an airtight container in a cool place.

PRIMROSE BAKERY

A couple of twirls and a backwards step from the Ceilidh Society, the blink-and-you'll-miss it Primrose Bakery was a champion of the cupcake revival in 2004. Founders Lisa Thomas and Martha Swift started life serving cupcakes from their home kitchens for children's parties and soon found a strong following, including famously Bono, Kate Moss and Jude Law.

Their home-focused, low volume production has allowed the Primrose Bakery to keep inventive, even now it has expanded beyond its original store with a new location in Covent Garden. Both have a few tables where you can sample the cakes with tea, coffee or a soft drink. In the Gloucester Avenue original, the colour comes from the cakes, as well as the pretty pastel hued room, a confection of pinks, greens and yellows with round tables reminiscent of 1950s' America. Cakes are arranged on stands and a blackboard displays the day's specials including ice-creams and Coke floats.

The cupcakes are all adorned with butter-cream icing, with the lemon cupcake a particular treat as well as unusual favourites such as their Earl Grey and Malted Marshmallow. Children will love the Batman and cute Hello Kitty varieties. That said, there's much more to the Primrose Bakery than the cupcakes. The caramel triple-layer cake is worth a detour, but really it is worth trying whatever is on offer. For kitchen-weary cooks, they do wonderful special occasion cakes including new baby and giant cupcakes. The shop welcomes children with open arms for tea, unlike some of the more upmarket hotels.

60 Gloucester Avenue, Primrose Hill, NW1 8LD · www.primrosebakery.org.uk · 020 7483 4222

THE RITZ

Arguably the home of the most famous tea in London – this is where Noel Coward penned some of his most famous songs, Tallulah Bankhead drank Champagne from her slipper, and King Edward VIII courted Wallis Simpson. Not much has changed since. The walls are still lavishly coated in 24-carat gold leaf; in fact much of the decor is exactly as it was when César Ritz opened the hotel in 1906. It is alleged that Mr. Ritz asked his wife to sit under the lights for hours on end until he found which was the most flattering for a woman – which makes it an imaginative place for a first date.

As well as a traditional or a Champagne tea, there is a Celebration Tea, beginning with a rendition of Happy Birthday on the grand piano by Ian Gomes, who once worked with Frank Sinatra. This is followed by a procession of liveried waiters bearing personalised birthday cakes. The menu has recently changed from offering treats with a French influence to one inspired by the hotel's British heritage. Smoked salmon is served with lemon-infused butter on rye bread; cheddar with sweet chutney on sticky onion bread. Apple and raisin scones are served warm, followed by an array of treats including Dundee cake, vanilla custard slice, raspberry and rosewater macaroons and Victoria sponge accompanied by a choice of 17 varieties of loose leaf tea. Saturdays are booked three months in advance. Still the place for a celebratory tea in London and one where you can safely take your Great Aunt and not expect any shocks.

150 Piccadilly, W1J 9BR · www.theritzlondon.com · 020 7493 8181

THE RITZ
Victoria Sponge

Serves 6-8	
Cake	Cream the butter, sugar and seeds of the vanilla pod until white and fluffy.
175g unsalted butter	
175g caster sugar	Add the eggs, continuously mixing, until totally incorporated.
3 eggs, beaten	This must be done very slowly or else the batter will split.
175g self-raising flour (sifted)	Add the sifted self-raising flour and combine.
1 vanilla pod	Pour into a greased and silicone paper lined cake tin.
Icing sugar to dust	
	Bake in a bakery oven at 200°C for 20 to 30 minutes and allow to cool.
Filling	Split the vanilla pod and scrape out the seeds.
200ml cream	
1 vanilla pod	To make the Chantilly cream, combine the cream, vanilla pod seeds
75g sugar	and sugar and whisk until good peaks appear.
100g strawberries	
100g strawberry jam	
To serve	Split the cooled sponge into two with a knife so you have two discs Open them.
	Spread the jam on one side of the sponge and top with sliced strawberries.
Make sure all ingredients are at ambient temperature.	Spread the Chantilly cream on top of the strawberries and jam, and place the other half of the sponge on top.
	Finish with sifted icing sugar.

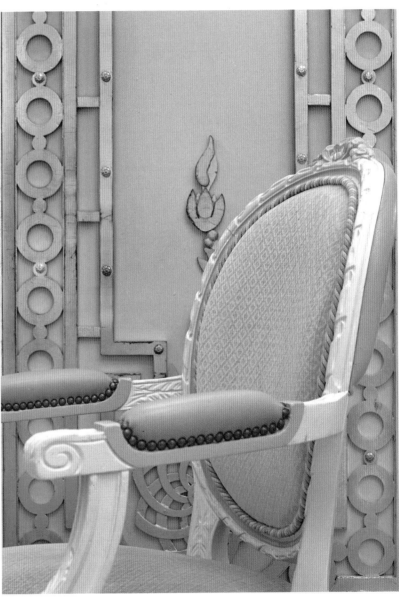

ROSE BAKERY

DOVER STREET MARKET

Rose Bakery sits on the fourth floor of Dover Street Market, the high-fashion department concept established by the founder of Comme des Garçons brand, Rei Kawakubo. Kawakubo wanted Dover Street Market to be the kind of place "where fashion becomes fascinating." As you make your way upstairs you are likely to agree that she certainly achieved that, with a concept that is almost intimidating in the meticulousness of its thrown-together pretension.

It's therefore a surprise to find such a low-key, welcoming café within such high fashion. Rose Carrarini set up the original Rose Bakery in Paris, and managed to make a great success of selling British baking and cooking to the French (with the help of her quiche-making husband, Jean-Charles). Kawakubo, Rose's sister-in-law, then invited Rose Bakery to cater for the Comme des Garçons show at Paris Fashion week. It was a short hop from there to Dover Street Market.

The crowd is a mixture of the fashionable and local Mayfair financiers, and you can enjoy a view of the rooftops of Mayfair over colourful salads. The emphasis is on simple, fresh, organic food. People rave about the bacon quiche and carrot cake, and the brownies and scones are also delicious.

Perhaps Kawakubo's inspiration for including the down-to-earth Rose Bakery within such high fashion was the Japanese proverb, "If a man has no tea in him, he's incapable of understanding truth and beauty." On the way down from Rose's after a sumptuous tea, the high fashion starts to make a lot more sense.

17-18 Dover Street, Mayfair, W1S 4LT · www.doverstreetmarket.com · 020 7518 0680

Carrot Cake

Serves 8

Cake

Unsalted butter, for greasing
4 eggs
225g caster sugar
300ml sunflower oil
4-5 medium carrots, finely grated
300g plain flour, sifted
1 tsp ground cinnamon
1 rounded tsp baking powder
½ tsp bicarbonate of soda
½ tsp salt
150g finely chopped walnuts

Preheat the oven to 180°C.

Butter a 23cm cake tin and line its base with parchment paper.

Beat the eggs and caster sugar until they are light and fluffy but not too white and meringue-like.

Pour in the oil and beat for a few more minutes.

Fold in the carrots and then the flour with the cinnamon, baking powder, bicarbonate of soda and salt. Finally fold in the walnuts.

Pour the mixture into the prepared tin and bake for about 45 minutes or until a knife inserted in the centre comes out clean.

Remove from the oven and cool the cake in the tin before taking it out.

Icing

125g unsalted butter, softened
250g cream cheese
½ tsp natural vanilla extract
50-75g icing sugar, depending on how sweet you like your icing

To make the icing, beat the butter with the cream cheese for a few minutes till the mixture is smooth.

Add the vanilla extract and icing sugar.

When the cake is cold, ice the top with the icing – it can be as smooth or rough as you like.

THE ROYAL ACADEMY OF ARTS

Even before you set eyes on any art, you're bound to be impressed by the magnificence of Burlington House, the home of the Royal Academy of Arts since 1867. But even though this building on Piccadilly started life as a private residence, grand buildings on this scale do not always make ideal settings for afternoon tea.

Sensing this challenge, the Royal Academy brought in restaurateur Oliver Peyton who had already created exciting restaurants in dramatic architectural settings. Working with interior designer Tom Dixon, he has created a room that has, at once, the sense of moment but fun. The splendid murals by Harold Speed, Fred Appleyard, Leonard Rosoman and Gilbert Spencer bring to life what could have been an austere room. An impressive glass installation houses sculptures from the permanent collection.

But alongside these are the cakes – a reminder that afternoon tea is central to the experience here and very much part of any gallery visit. You can buy cakes individually – the selection changes daily but classics such as fig roll and the excellent carrot cake are often to be found. But you might want to opt for one of the afternoon teas. The classic afternoon tea would suit the traditionalist looking for scones, finger sandwiches and cakes but the special teas created to tie in with exhibitions such as the Degas tea with foie gras and San Daniele ham or the Yorkshire Tea for the Hockney exhibition with trout, Filey Bay crab and roast Yorkshire beef sandwiches might be more in keeping with the richness on display within the room.

Burlington House, Piccadilly, W1J 0BD · www.royalacademy.org.uk · 020 7300 5608

SANDERSON

The Courtyard Restaurant inside a cutting edge Philippe Starck designed hotel may not be the most obvious choice for an Alice in Wonderland inspired tea, but it is definitely one of the most fun in London and brilliant for children, or just the inner child in all of us. It is also the most inventive – where else can you get lollipops, ice-cream and mini potion bottles on a sleepy afternoon? You can choose to take it on the blond wood benches inside, which has a utilitarian, clean, slightly austere feeling. However for a more escapist environment, head to the garden instead with its calming water features and lush greenery. The tea, which comes on a multilayered mismatched cake stand begins with some exquisite sandwiches with conventional fillings such as smoked salmon or egg and cress but it is the colourful breads – including beetroot and saffron – that add the element of fun and play on the senses. There are hot and cold lollipops, a choc-ice bombe, a fabulous Drink Me potion consisting of coconut pannacotta, passion fruit jelly and a fruity foam, and a delectable strawberry Eat Me heart-shaped cake. Scones are crumbly, and come with lashings of clotted cream and jam. There are seasonal adjustments to the menu, such as mini mince pies during the festive period. The tea comes with a glass of Champagne – the tea itself merely an afterthought with more focus on cocktails. And after tea it's a mere hop to the Long Bar to while away the rest of the afternoon keeping up with the City boys on their Martini marathons.

50 Berners Street, Fitzrovia, W1T 3NG · www.sandersonlondon.com · 020 7300 1400

THE SAVOY

One of the original homes of the tango teas and *thés dansants* the elegant Thames Foyer is still home to late-night dancing and there is a resident pianist during the day. Built by the impresario Richard D'Oyly Carte on the proceeds of his productions of Gilbert & Sullivan, opened in 1889 and renovated in 2010, the Savoy is where Churchill chose to have impromptu cabinet lunches. Illustrious guests have included Marilyn Monroe, Fred Astaire, Elizabeth Taylor, Laurence Olivier, Frank Sinatra Jimmy Hendrix and Elton John. A newly restored glass cupola floods the room below with natural light; it is here that guests were once dropped off in their horse-drawn carriages. Now, designed by Pierre-Yves Rochon, this is a quiet retreat from Covent Garden in which to take tea. It starts with sandwiches such as Scottish smoked salmon and horseradish and honey-roast ham with apple cider mustard. After scones with clotted cream and strawberry jam, there is a table side service offering French pastries such as vanilla lavender éclairs and raspberry and passionfruit macaroons. Finally, the indulgence ends with cakes ranging from traditional English fruitcake to carrot cake with orange icing. On Sundays there is a Decadence Tea, which includes 'tipsy' drinks, taken in the Art Deco gold and black Beaufort Bar. Delicious handmade treats and loose-leaf teas can be bought from the tea shop situated in the upper Thames Foyer where you can also watch the pastry chefs and chocolatiers hard at work.

Strand, Holborn, WC2R 0EU · www.fairmont.com · 020 7836 4343

Vanilla Lavender Éclair

Makes 200

Choux pastry (200pcs)

1lt water
500g butter
60g sugar
15g salt
1000g strong flour
1000g whole eggs (20)

Bring the water, butter, sugar and salt to the boil.
Add flour and cook out until it comes clean from the pan.
Put on a machine with a beater speed 2 and
slowly add the eggs whilst it is still hot.
Pipe individual éclairs onto a baking sheet
Bake: 180°C-200°C then lower temperature later until dry.
Note: open damp when it puffs.

Pastry cream

3000g milk
4 vanilla pods
20g vanilla flavour
600g egg yolks (30)
450g sugar
240g cornflour
600g butter

Boil the milk and the vanilla.
Mix the egg yolks with sugar and then add the cornflour.
Pour some boiling milk onto the egg mixture, return it
to the pan and re-boil.
Spread on a tray lined with plastic and cover with another
sheet of plastic.

Lavender syrup

250g water
250g sugar
2.5ml scoop of lavender flowers

Boil and pass through a sieve.

Lavender fondant

500g fondant icing
80g lavender syrup
2 drops of colour

Combine and warm to 30°C.

Crystallised lavender

Lavender flowers
Egg white
Sugar

Very lightly coat the lavender
flowers with egg white and sugar
and dry in a warm place.

Fill the éclairs with the pastry cream, ice with the fondant
and decorate with the crystallised lavender flowers.

SHAKESPEARE'S GLOBE

For a Bankside pedestrian at the end of the sixteenth century, the Swan would have brought to mind the Swan Theatre. Nowadays, theatre people flock to the reconstructed Globe, and the Swan bar and restaurant sit beside it serving drinks and food throughout the day – the perfect stopping point en route from Tate Modern.

Afternoon Teas are served both in the lively downstairs bar and the quieter upstairs restaurant. While sharing a table downstairs can be fun, a table upstairs by the window offers magnificent views of St. Paul's across the Thames and a chance to reflect as the tourist throngs mill below.

With good food throughout the day, the emphasis is more on Elizabethan than Victorian dining, with relaxed service and generous portions. There's more than a nod to the locally sourcing epitomised by nearby Borough Market. There is a traditional Afternoon Tea served on weekdays and also a Gentleman's High Tea, complete with Berkshire bangers, (onion) bread with fish fingers, smoked bacon, macaroni cheese, brownies with brandy cream accompanied by (London Pride) beer. If that's too masculine for you, the Afternoon Tea offers a more traditional selection of Wiltshire ham, smoked salmon, and beef finger sandwiches, cakes and scones, and of course, tea!

21 New Globe Walk, South Bank, SE1 9DT · www.shakespearesglobe.com · 020 7928 9444

Parkin

Makes 12

230g softened butter

450g flour

2 tsp bicarbonate soda

4 tsp ground ginger

2 tsp ground cinnamon

2 tsp mixed spice

1g salt

110g coarse oatmeal

350g dark sugar

170g golden syrup

280g black treacle

300ml milk at room temperature

2 eggs

Mix all the dry ingredients together in a bowl and add the milk and the softened butter.

In a separate dish, whisk the dark sugar and eggs together before adding the golden syrup and black treacle.

Now combine all the ingredients together into one bowl.

Pour the mixture into a greased cake tin and cook at 140°C for approximately 30 minutes.

When cooked, leave to cool before slicing.

Best served with a chunk of Cashel Blue or another good quality blue cheese.

SKETCH

If you want your lampshades to be made of twigs, your teacups to be rubber and your loos to be futuristic white pods, but still get one of the best tasting teas in London – this is the place to come. The vision of madcap Algerian restaurateur Mourad Mazouz, as well as housing Pierre Gagnaire's Michelin starred restaurant upstairs, Sketch includes two rooms on the ground floor where tea can be taken. The Parlour operates a no bookings policy at teatime – and is often full to capacity – but once you are in you are free to join the surrealists' teaparty. With typical Mazouz flourishes the furniture is a mishmash of Louis XV seating, lampshades decorated with skulls, and décor that has something of the chic brothel about it. It is warming, fun and loungy, the perfect environment in which to spend a few hours feasting on the quirky but incredibly good pastries on offer. The madeleines filled with jam are a great accompaniment to the tea which comes in playful Polly George crockery. Do not miss the opportunity to indulge in the full afternoon tea, complete with wonderful scones and dainty cakes – proving that you can mix style and substance. If the Parlour is full then from 6pm the Glade downstairs offers a fantasy retreat – with its twiggy lampshades, Swarovski encrusted bar and haunting live singers.

9 Conduit Street, Mayfair, W1S 2XG · www.sketch.uk.com · 020 7659 4500

Madeleines

Serves 45

240g fresh eggs
217g caster sugar
80g acacia honey
100g milk
333g butter
2g salt
17g baking powder
333g flour T55

Heat the milk, butter and honey in a saucepan at 55°C.

Mix the eggs and the sugar very slowly.

Add half of the warm liquid, mix well and then add the flour, baking powder and salt.

Add the rest of the warm liquid and mix well until homogeneous.

Butter a madeleine tin with a pastry brush.

Pour in the mixture.

Bake in a preheated oven at 180°C for 8-9 minutes.

THE SOHO HOTEL

Located in an alleyway off Dean Street, the Soho Hotel is buzzy and busy and you can see why it is where all the local film industry folk like to come for a wind-down after work: Kit Kemp combines eye-catching pieces of art, such as the huge Fernando Botero sculpture in the lobby, with huge urns of flowers and kooky displays of 1950s gasoline tins in the bar, Refuel, where you can take afternoon tea. For a more genteel approach, head to the Drawing Room. With its fireplaces, deep sofas and chessboards this is designed for relaxing. There is also a third option – the Library, which has a more classic feel. Surrounded by works by cartographer Jean-Baptiste Nolin and artist François Bard, sip on Pommery Champagne while enjoying delicious chocolate fudge cake, apple tart and glazed ham and mustard sandwiches. If you time it right you can combine tea in Refuel with a lazy afternoon of watching an old classic or recently released film as part of the group's Saturday Film Club. Films are included in the price of the afternoon tea and are screened in their private cinema. They start at 3.30pm. Recent screenings have included *It's a Wonderful Life*, *Sleeping Beauty* and *The Help*.

4 Richmond Mews, Soho, W1D 3DH · www.firmdale.com · 020 7559 3000

Soholistic

Serves 1

6 red berries plus 1 raspberry for garnish

50ml Finlandia vodka

15ml Crème de Cassis

40ml cranberry juice

5ml lemon juice

Muddle berries.

Add the rest of ingredients.

Shake and strain into a long glass on crushed ice.

Garnish with one raspberry.

THE SPATISSERIE

THE DORCHESTER

For some spa goers, the idea of relaxing after a triple oxygen facial means a wheatgrass smoothie. However, for those who like a bit of indulgence, the white room adjoining the spa is the perfect place in which to unwind after a treatment in the Carol Joy spa – or just the place for a quiet catch-up with girlfriends.

Designed by Fox Linton and opened in 2009, the interiors are a beautiful mix of white and pink – with white muslin curtains, elegant upholstered chairs and a crystal central table supporting bowls of fruit and cakes. The tea menu is extremely extensive. Broken down into sections, from Delicate and Scented, including Sencha and Arabian Mint, to distinctive Black teas such as Russian Country and Keemun. There are also cleansing teas such as nettle and fennel. There is the same Champagne tea on offer as in The Promenade Restaurant upstairs. This includes finger sandwiches, scones, pastries and a glass of Champagne. If, however, you subscribe to their ethos of 'a little bit of what you fancy does you good,' then you can order individual sugary delights and the chocolate mudcake is enough to convince even the most hardened spa goer that cocoa has therapeutic properties. No spa appointment is necessary for a teatime booking. For a day of total indulgence, hen party or baby shower, you can reserve the whole room – which holds eighteen.

Park Lane, Mayfair, W1K 1QA · www.thedorchester.com · 020 7317 6501

TEASMITH

This zen-like temple to tea is for those who are interested in taking the afternoon brew to geeky heights. From sourcing the leaves from craft producers, to making sure each leaf is brewed in a pot of appropriate shape and at the correct temperature to enhance its characteristics, this establishment is run by people who are passionate about tea. In design it is as far from a classic English tearoom as is possible, with its Japanese-inspired clean lines and utilitarian feel. Tea aficionados can perch at the tea bar and learn about their dizzying range of teas and how to distinguish between a Darjeeling 2nd flush and an Xtra Old Tippy Puer. The tea is brewed in front of you (each one infused at least three times) by knowledgeable teasmiths who will explain how to create the perfect cup of tea. However, if all this sounds like hard work and you would prefer a less pedagogic approach, then just relax and enjoy some of the sweet treats made for the shop by master chocolatier William Curley. Perhaps the sweet and salty walnut and miso biscuit, a chocolate yuzu cake, or some delicate jasmine truffles. There are masterclasses to teach you how to recreate the perfect cup of tea at home, and most of the teas are available to buy. There are also tea and chocolate pairing events for those who prefer something a bit more interesting than a custard cream with their tea.

6 Lamb Street, Shoreditch, E1 6EA · www.teasmith.co.uk · 020 7247 1333

YAUATCHA

For an eastern inspired tea, look no further than dim-sum destination Yauatcha – part of the same stable as hip Chinese fusion restaurant Hakkasan and recently opened Ni Ju San. Although it doesn't serve an afternoon tea as such, their cakes and macaroons, displayed beautifully in glass cabinets at the front of the restaurant, are mini works of art and perfect if you want a sugar hit without a calorie-rich full afternoon tea. Choose from a dizzying array of brightly hued cakes from pumpkin gingerbread to a glorious raspberry délice or a minty coconut charlotte. The room is designed with calm in mind – a huge blue fish tank covers one wall. Staff work with quiet efficiency, even the dim sum chefs who work from an open kitchen at the back of the upstairs restaurant. The back wall is covered with large tins selling a huge array of loose-leaf teas. The pink and purple menus guide you through the dizzying range of teas, from delicately scented blue teas to dark and green teas – best paired with one or two of the dainty and almost gaudily-coloured macaroons. Or you can always pep yourself up with one of their famously moreish cocktails – and even imagine you are drinking tea, with one of their Oolong tea based cocktails. It is hard to leave without taking a little something home, even if it is simply for the gorgeous pink, grey and mint green boxes. If you have had your fill of cakes you can buy any of their extensive range of loose-leaf teas, or incense sticks including lemongrass and ginger.

15-17 Broadwick Street, Soho, W1F 0DL · www.yauatcha.com · 020 7494 8888

Vanilla Macaroon & Tonka Ganache

Makes 30

Vanilla macaroon

250g ground almonds

250g icing sugar

90g fresh egg whites
(24 hours at room temperature)

250g sugar

75ml water

90g fresh egg whites
(24 hours at room temperature)

1g egg white powder

1 vanilla pod, scraped

Sieve the ground almonds and icing sugar and mix well.

Mix 90g fresh egg whites with the mixture to make a temps per temps.

Semi-whip the remaining 90g of egg whites, the egg white powder and the vanilla seeds. Add the sugar to the water, bring to the boil and allow to heat to 121°C. Pour over the semi-whipped egg whites, whisking all the time, until the mixture is cool. This makes a firm, silky meringue.

Fold the meringue through the temps per temps.

Beat until slightly slackened.

Pipe onto paper-lined trays and leave until a skin forms (about 30 minutes).

Bake at 180°C for about 7 minutes.

Turn the tray, and bake for an additional 3 minutes, or until the macaroon comes easily off the paper.

Tonka ganache

250g whipping cream

225g dark chocolate, roughly chopped

25g Trimoline

90g soft butter

5 grated Tonka beans

Boil the cream with the grated Tonka beans and infuse for 10 minutes.

Pass the cream and pour it onto the chocolate pieces and Trimoline.

Cool to 55°C.

Blitz the butter into the mix and leave overnight to set.

To serve

Sandwich two macaroons together with the Tonka ganache.

Jean Cazals

Jean Cazals is an award-winning food photographer living in London where he has worked for the past ten years with publishers, advertising and design clients. He lives in Notting Hill with his wife and daughter.

His work has appeared in *House & Garden*, *Delicious*, *Food & Travel*, *ELLE*, *Marie Claire*, *Condé Nast Traveller*, *Vogue Entertaining*, *Martha Stewart Living*, *The Sunday Times*, *The Telegraph Magazine* and *Olive*.

In addition, his work has been published in over 70 cookbooks and he has worked with numerous international chefs including Michel Roux, Peter Gordon, Jamie Oliver, Gordon Ramsey, J.P. Hévin, Raymond Blanc, Ken Hom, Paul Bocuse and Alain Ducasse.

His books include *MoMo*, *The Savoy*, *The Cinnamon Club*, *Le Gavroche*, *The Square*, *Chez Bruce*, *Cuisiner Gascon* (best French cookbook 2010), *La Cuisine des Brasseries* (Prix Gourmand 2004), *Dough* (Glenfiddich best photo nominee 2006), *Crust* (James Beard best photo nominee 2008), *Cinnamon Club Seafood* (best seafood book UK 2006) and *Melt* (best chocolate book UK 2010).